# HISTORY OF THE
# LANCASHIRE FOOTBALL ASSOCIATION

## 1878—1928.

Published by:
**Yore Publications,**
12, The Furrows, Harefield,
Middlesex. UB9 6AT.

© Yore Publications 1992

**British Library Cataloguing-in-Publication Data**
A catalogue record for this book is available from the British Library.

ISBN 1 874427 10 0

Printed by:
Bath Press Ltd.

Yore Publications would like to express their thanks to the Lancashire Football Associaion for their co-operation in making this reprint possible.

# HISTORY

*of*

# The Lancashire Football Association

## 1878—1928.

*Compiled by*

C. E. SUTCLIFFE, President,

*and*

F. HARGREAVES, Secretary.

BLACKBURN:
GEO. TOULMIN & SONS, LTD.,
THE TIMES PRINTING WORKS,
1928.

LANCASHIRE F.A. COUNCIL AT LYTHAM, 15th AUGUST, 1928.

Back Row: E. A. Morton, J.P.; R. A. Beeley, T. A. Barcroft, H. Duckworth, J. Taylor.
Third Row: W. J. Sawyer, J. W. Walsh, T. P. Campbell, W. Cooper (Clerk).
Second Row: H. P. Hardman, C. E. Foweraker, H. Windle, W. E. Bracewell, W. Dickinson, J. Kenny, F. Morris, J. W. Haworth, E. C. Witter, J.P.
Front Row: T. Laithwaite (Hon. Treas.), E. Little (Vice-President), C. E. Sutcliffe (President), R. Watson (Vice-President), T. Y. Ritson (Vice-President). F. Hargreaves (Secretary).

# Foreword To The 1992 Reprint Edition

❖❖❖❖❖❖❖❖❖❖❖❖❖❖❖❖❖❖❖❖❖

It is a privilege to make a small contribution to the re–printing of: 'The History of The Lancashire Football Association 1878 – 1928'.

This book provides some wonderfully detailed information from the inception of the Association which the reader will find absorbing and fascinating.

At our Centenary celebration held at the Imperial Hotel, Blackpool, during September 1978, many glowing tributes were paid to the stirling service of our early and legendary football administrators. Testimony of their firm foundation of the Association is borne in today's thriving establishment some 114 years later.

The Lancashire Football Association is immensely proud of its past and now faces the 21st Century with confidence which reflects the depth and enduring popularity of the game of football.

The President, Council and Staff are sure that all who pick up the book will find our first fifty years compulsive reading

...................................

**J.Kenyon, Secretary**
**Lancashire Football Association**

# CONTENTS.

# LIST OF ILLUSTRATIONS.

B

# FOREWORD.

The History of the Lancashire Football Association is largely the history of its Clubs, and to attempt to write such a history and maintain its completeness within the pages available for the purpose would be impossible, and so there must be compression and omission, yet it is hoped that this record may be both instructive and interesting. When one sets out to recall the prominent incidents and noteworthy events the first problem is where to start, and then comes the difficulty where to leave off. To make the history interesting many will look for quantity, others for quality. Probably neither will be able to find all they wish, yet may find many acceptable reminiscences which will recall many happy memories. Those who have had a long association in the game, we doubt not at the mention of past players and governors of the game, will remember days gone by with pleasure. To those who have come recently into the game or its government we can only hope that this history will prove an inspiration.

The Association, which at the outset was merely a Club representation with small powers and less experience, tainted at times with political, and at others with local associations, has grown into an organisation which simply lives for football in the County. The days of ornamental officers were comparatively few, but out of the simplicity of government and control, a Council of Governors with a thorough knowledge and experience of the game has been evolved. With the Marquess of Hartington as its first President and other officers of local repute, but with little association of the game, its government was bound to be primitive, but the Association gradually changed in character until to-day there is no room, and less use, for Councillors who are not thoroughly versed in all phases of football government.

The Lancashire Football Association, though not the first County Organisation to be formed in the game, soon took the position of pre-eminence, and we may to-day justly and proudly claim that it is one of, if not the most, important and best conducted and controlled organisations in the game. The evolution of the County Association must be traced through the history of many Clubs that have ceased to operate long ago, yet, how could the Association have been formed and grown in strength but for such Clubs as Blackburn Olympic, Witton, Park Road, Accrington. Church, Haslingden, Turton, Eagley, Bootle, Higher Walton, Astley Bridge, Great Lever, Halliwell Rovers, Fishwick Ramblers, and South Shore. Clubs that are now only a memory, yet there would have been no Lancashire Football Association, and may we say with modesty, no Football League, but for the foundation these Clubs laid.

To-day a history of the game of The Football Association, or of The Football League, would be incomplete without repeated reference to our County Association.

It is a matter of pride that at its Jubilee the Lancashire Football Association is better and sounder than ever in its history. For its pride of place the credit and honour belong to the pioneers who digged the foundation and gradually built the super-structure. Fortunately, the Association has had the advantage of long interest of many of its Councillors, and amongst the honoured names connected with the game, Lancashire has given its quota and as we unravel the story of progress in Club and County, we would remind all readers that the credit of the game to-day belongs to the Clubs and Governors of the past, for we reap as they have sown.

C. E. SUTCLIFFE (*President*).

# THE ORIGIN, RISE, AND GROWTH OF THE LANCASHIRE FOOTBALL ASSOCIATION.

## CHAPTER I.—EARLY FOOTBALL,

*Turton F.C. Birth of Lancashire F.A. Fixture Making. County Matches. Marquess of Hartington First President, Mr. W. Forrest the Second President, Mr. T. Hindle the First Secretary, his resignation, Mr. R. P. Gregson appointed. Growth of activities. Mr. D. B. Woolfall elected President. Full-time Secretary decided upon. Mr. F. Hargreaves appointed.*

T HERE is an amount of evidence of organised football being played in the North of England so far back as 1871, the matches being conducted under what were known as the Harrow Rules, later in 1874 the Rules of the London F.A. were adopted by Turton F.C.

In 1876 Turton F.C. in arranging their fixtures agreed to play Darwen F.C., subject to " the match being played according to the Association Rules as interpreted by the London Association " and " that this match be ' off ' if a satisfactory answer as to ' hands ' be not obtained from the Darwen Hon. Secretary." It will therefore be seen that Turton F.C. became not only the pioneer, but a jealous guardian of the right interpretation of the Rules.

New Clubs were formed in various districts, particularly in Blackburn, Bolton, and Darwen. One of these was Bolton Christ Church, which ultimately became Bolton Wanderers. The Turton F.C. became Members of The F.A. in 1876, from which it will be seen that the Club believed in affiliation and organisation, and it is worthy of note that there were connected with that Club, officials and players who not only helped to make Turton F.C. noted and popular, but who later gave their services in connection with many football organisations, J. J. Bentley, W. T. Dixon, J. J. Haworth, Richard Birtwistle and John Booth, being all associated with the Village Club. Little wonder that this desire for control and co-ordination found expression in the formation of a Lancashire Association, and that the first steps should be taken near to Turton.

The origin of the Lancashire F.A. was due to a meeting held one Sunday afternoon in the old fashioned parlour of the Volunteer Inn, Bromley Cross, the time and venue is all the more surprising in view of the fact that the late John Lewis—a fearless advocate of teetotalism—was one of the party, the others being the late T. Hindle, of Darwen, and W. T. Dixon, Secretary of Turton F.C. It was at the meeting referred to, that the *modus operandi* was discussed, and arrangements made for a representative meeting of Clubs to be held. On pages 27-29 is to be found a record of that first memorable meeting held on 28th September, 1878, at which was formed the Lancashire F.A., which as events proved, became a great factor and influence, not merely in arranging matches, and fostering Association football, but in guiding and leading the Clubs of England when the titanic struggle of professionalism was fought and won.

As already indicated the early work of the Association was that of arranging matches for its Clubs. That may appear to many a very simple and insignificant operation, but an examination of the Minute books reveal that which is not otherwise apparent. Fifty years ago Clubs were just as anxious as now to arrange matches at home on certain dates, and the Association Minutes indicate many of the disputes in regard to the fixtures; again, very many meetings were held to deal with protests as to the eligibility of players, players' residential qualifications, and protests as to payment of players. The payments of players sub-rosa became a scandal, and it was generally known that certain Clubs kept duplicate sets of books to avoid detection.

**THE MARQUESS OF HARTINGTON,**
First President of the Association, 1878-1889.

The Association not merely settled protests and disputes, but also organised many games, which in those days were looked upon as great events. Matches were played with various Counties, amongst them being :—

| | | |
|---|---|---|
| Ayrshire. | Glasgow. | Sheffield. |
| Birmingham. | London. | Staffordshire. |
| Cleveland. | Nottingham. | Sussex. |
| Dumbarton. | North Wales. | United Ulster |
| East of Scotland. | Northumberland. | |

In 1879 the Senior Cup Competition was established, and that in itself provided an abundance of work.

The disputes or "wrangles" between Blackburn Rovers v. Darwen, Accrington v. Preston North End, elsewhere referred to at length, were strenuous and prolonged struggles which might have wrecked the Association. In 1885-86 the Junior Cup Competition was formed, thereby giving a stimulus to Clubs crowded out of the Senior Competition.

In 1884 the fight on the legalisation of professionalism occurred. (See pages 147-155 for a special review of this matter).

The first President of the Association was the Marquess of Hartington, who later became the Duke of Devonshire, and he retained that Office until 1889. At the Annual Meeting held in April, 1886, a spirited attempt was made to remove His Lordship from the Presidency. Mr. J. S. Roscow, of Great Lever, one of the straightest men ever connected with the game, moved that Mr. William Forrest be elected President, that was seconded by Mr. J. Booth, who remarked, "Lord Hartington never did them any good, either there or anywhere else," and Mr. Roscow declared, " the day was passed for ornamental officers," however, Mr. Forrest declined to oppose Lord Hartington, and the latter remained President for a further two Seasons, when the malcontents won their way.

Mr. William Forrest was President from 1889 to 1901

The first Secretary of the Association was Mr. T Hindle, of Darwen, who held the post for almost four years. Mr. W. T. Dixon, of Turton, being the Treasurer.

Mr. Hindle's resignation as Secretary caused the live-liest competition for the post. There were 18 applications, and the last four were Messrs. J. J. Bentley, Bolton ; W. Bramham, Blackburn ; R. P. Gregson, Blackburn ; and Tom Heald, Accrington. The third named was event-ually elected, the final vote being, Gregson 32, Bentley 13. Mr. Gregson held the office until he retired in 1911.

In 1893-94 the Amateur Cup Competition was formed, thereby supplying the needs of Clubs distinct from pro-fessional Clubs, yet of a higher status than most Junior and Amateur organisations.

The "nineties" do not show any marked develop-ment or any special work performed by the Association.

There were 74 Clubs in Membership with the Association in 1898-99, and though there were a few local Leagues in existence there was very little control and super-vision. The outward correspondence was only 3,000 per year, and it will therefore be realised that the post of Secretary was only a part time appointment.

The following statistics indicate the rapid growth of the Association.

| | Clubs. | Leagues. | Outward Correspon- dence. | Referees. | Discip- line Cases. |
|---|---|---|---|---|---|
| 1907-08 | 203 | 35 | 4,300 | 345 | 481 |
| 1910-11 | 232 | 38 | 8,400 | 590 | 540 |
| 1914-15 | 178 | 50 | 10,200 | 600 | 600 |

Then came the Great War, its clash of arms, its clarion call to the manhood of the Country. True, football was played under War-time conditions, but the years 1915-1918 can never be quoted for records or comparisions. Whole organisations—Clubs and Leagues—disappeared, players enlisted in hundreds. Prior to conscription a register was kept of Lancashire footballers who joined the Colours, and it numbered 4,765 when the present Secretary of the Asso-ciation was accepted for service, after having been rejected on several occasions, and with his enlistment no further record was kept.

**W. FORREST.**
Second President of the Association.
1889-1901.

**D. B. WOOLFALL.**
Third President of the Association.
1901-1918.
Elected to Council 1881.

**J. LEWIS.**
Fourth President of the Association.
1901-1926.
Elected to Council 1889, after one
year in 1878.

**W. T. DIXON.**
First Hon. Treasurer of the Association.
1878-1882.

**J. S. ROSCOW.**
Vice-President of the Association.
1901-1918.
Elected to Council 1884.

**T. HINDLE.**
First Secretary of the Association,
1878-1882, and
Second Hon. Treasurer, 1882-1919.

**T. DUXBURY.**
Vice-President of the Association.
1889-1904.

**J. J. BENTLEY.**
Vice-President of the Association.
1901-1918.
Elected to Council, 1887.

Immediately after the Armistice in 1918, the Council of the Lancashire F.A. met to review the position, and a Reconstruction Committee was appointed, and the work of re-organisation proceeded with. The results were highly gratifying, and in an incredibly short time the following figures were announced.

| Clubs. | Associates. | Leagues. | Outward corres- pondence. | Referees. |
|---|---|---|---|---|
| 1919-20 92 | 118 | 40 | 10,498 | 380 |
| 1921-22 94 | 340 | 74 | 17,381 | 991 |

The control of 74 leagues gives jurisdiction over 2,000 clubs.

From 1901 to 1918 Mr. D. B. Woolfall was President of the Association, during which period he was assisted by Messrs. J. J. Bentley, J. J. Cooper, J. S. Roscow, J. Lewis, T. Duxbury, W. E. Ord, A. E. Heap, T. Houghton, W. A. Duckworth, Isaac Smith, R. Iddon, R. B. Falla, James Cooper, D. Porteous, R. H. Wadge, W. Heath, J. A. McGregor, J. J. Haworth, R. B. Middleton, all of whom have passed over to the great majority; other Members who served under Mr. Woolfall, and who are still connected with the Association, are Mr. C. E. Sutcliffe (the present President), Messrs. J. McKenna, R. Watson, R. E. Lythgoe, R. Birtwistle, T. Y. Ritson, E. Little, T. Laithwaite, T. A. Barcroft, T. P. Campbell, J. Taylor, and W. Dickinson.

The development of the game made it imperative for a full time Secretary to be appointed, and on 26th April, 1911, Mr. F. Hargreaves was unanimously elected. The post was not thrown open for competition, the reason no doubt being that Mr. Hargreaves had been associated with his predecessor since 1900, and that from 1903 until 1911 he had been in close touch with the work of the Association and in attendance at meetings ; in fact, in 1908 he was elected Registrar of Referees, which post was later combined with the Secretary's general duties.

## DARWEN F.C.

FIRST WINNERS OF THE LANCASHIRE CUP, 1879-80.

J. Duxbury, S. Fish, W. Brindle, L. Broughton, W. H. Moorehouse.
T. Marshall, T. Rostron, Dr. Gledhill, Dr. J. C. Holden, R. Kirkham, T. Bury.
F. Suter.

# CHAPTER II.

## COPY OF THE MINUTES OF THE FIRST MEETING OF THE ASSOCIATION.

September 28th, 1878.

A Meeting of the Association Football Clubs of Lanca-shire called by Thos. Hindle acting on behalf of the Darwen C. and Football Club, was held in the Conversation Room, Co-operative Hall, Darwen, to consider the advisability of forming a Lancashire Football Association.

The following Clubs sent two representatives to the Meeting, viz., Astley Bridge, Cloughfold, Blackburn Rovers, Park Road, Livesey United, St. Mark's, Blackburn St. George's, Christ Church, Bolton Rovers, Bolton St. George's, Emmanuel, Bolton Wanderers, Great Lever, North End, Eagley, Turton, Church, Enfield, Darwen, Darwen Rangers, Lower Darwen, Haslingden Rangers, Grange.

Mr. Thos. Hindle was voted to the Chair.

Thos. Duxbury (Darwen), moved, and T. Dixon (Turton), seconded, that this meeting considers it advisable and expedient to form a Lancashire Football Association, and pledges itself to take the necessary steps to attain that object.

The Motion was then put to the Meeting and carried unanimously.

The following Rules were then submitted to the Meeting by the Chairman and unanimously carried :—

Rule 1.—That the Association be called the Lancashire Football Association.

Rule 2.—That all Clubs playing Lancashire Association Rules be eligible for Membership, subject to the approval of the Committee of the Association.

Rule 3.—That the Subscription for each Club be 10/6 per annum, payable in September or within one week after joining, and if further calls be requisite, that a General Meeting of Representatives be called to consider the subject.

Rule 4.—That the Officers be a President, two Vice-Presidents, Treasurer and a Secretary with a Committee, comprising the above mentioned Officers, and one member from each club, and elected by that club; five to form a quorum.  It shall be in the power of the Committee to appoint one of their body to act as Assistant Secretary if necessary.

Rule 5.—That the Officers be elected from, and by the representatives of Clubs present at the Annual Meeting, the retiring Officers to be eligible for re-election.  That no club shall have more than two representatives on the Committee.

Rule 6.—That the Annual Meeting be held in ———— (place to be decided upon at first Committee Meeting for this Year) in the first week in September.

Rule 7.—That each club be entitled to appoint two re-presentatives to attend all general meetings of the Association.  No two clubs to be represented by the same individual.

Rule 8.—That in the event of any alteration being deemed necessary in the Rules of the Association, or Laws of the Game, notices of the proposed alterations shall be sent in writing to the Secretary, on or before the 1st August and the Secretary shall inform each club of the proposed alteration on or before the 15th August.

Rule 9—That each club shall forward its name, the date when formed, the name and address of its Secretary and a statement of its distinguishing colours or costume, the situation of their ground, etc., to the Secretary of the Association.

Rule 10.—That all clubs belonging to the Association shall play the Rules of the Association, and any club failing to comply shall cease to be members thereof.

Rule 11.—That any club competing for any prize offered by any private individual or individuals, unless the net proceeds go to some Football club or clubs, or Charity or Charities, shall cease to be members of this Association.

Rule 12.—That the Committee shall have power to call special General Meetings as they may deem necessary.

It was moved, seconded and carried that the Rules and Laws of the Game of the English Association should apply to this Association.

It was moved, seconded and carried that Thos. Hindle (Darwen), be appointed Hon. Secretary for the Season, and W. T. Dixon (Turton), Hon. Treasurer.

It was resolved that the Secretary send out circulars to the clubs joining the Association requesting them to appoint a representative to sit on the Committee on their behalf and send in his name and address to him.

It was resolved that the Committee have power to elect the President and Vice-Presidents for this Season at their first meeting.

It was resolved that the Rules and Laws of the Game be printed, also giving the names of the clubs members of this Association with other particulars.

The following Clubs were the first members of the Association, Astley Bridge, Blackburn Rovers, Blackburn Christ Church, Livesey United, Blackburn Park Road, Blackburn St. George', Blackburn St. Mark's, Bolton Emmanuel, Bolton North End, Bolton Wanderers, Bolton St. George's, Bolton Rovers, Bolton St. Paul's, Church, Clough Fold, Myrtle Grove, Darwen, Lower Darwen, Darwen Grasshoppers, Darwen Rangers, Darwen Lower Chapel, Darwen St. James, Eagley, Enfield, Great Lever, Haslingden Rangers, Haslingden Grane, Turton.

## LIST OF VICE-PRESIDENTS.

The following list contains many illustrious names, and the names awaken many memories.

1878-86.  W. Y. Hargreaves (Bolton).

1878-79.  R. H. Ainsworth (Bolton).

1880-84.  T. Milne, M.D. (Accrington).

1880-82.  J. N. Boothman (Blackburn).

1881-82.  T R. Haslam (Great Lever).

1881.  J. Kerr (Church).

1882-89.  W. Forrest (Turton).

1882-84.  E. S. Morley, M.D. (Blackburn).

1884-85.  J. Johnston, J.P. (Blackburn).

1884-88.  J. Bullough (Accrington).

1885-1901.  D. B. Woolfall (Blackburn).

1886-93.  W. Sudell (Preston).

1886-89.  J. Bowness (Newchurch).

1888-89.  C. J. Massey (Burnley).

1889-1904.  T. Duxbury (Darwen).

1889-1901.  S. Ormerod (Accrington).

1889-1919.  J. J. Cooper (Pleasington).

1893-95.  J. Bickerstaff (Blackpool).

1895-1901.  R. Iddon (Higher Walton).

1901-1918.  J. S. Roscow (Bolton).

1901-1918.  J. J. Bentley (Bolton).

1901-1918.  J. Lewis (Blackburn.

1904-1922.  W. E. Ord (Preston).

1918-1926.  C. E. Sutcliffe (Rawtenstall)

1918.  J. McKenna (Liverpool).

1918.  R. Watson (Accrington).

1919.  R. Birtwistle (Blackburn).

1922.  R. E. Lythgoe (Liverpool).

1926.  T. Y. Ritson (Bolton).

1927.  E. Little (Blackpool).

## TURTON F.C.

### WINNERS OF JUNIOR CUP, 1901-2.

J. Derbyshire, C. Lill, J. Whittle, H. Walker.

J. W. Theckston (Trainer), F. Haworth (Reserve), P. Cannon, H. Tyrer, S. Greenhalgh, A. Ramsden (Secretary).

J. Booth, J. Jones, W. Lomax (Reserve), G. R. Booth, R. Whitehead.

# CHAPTER III.

## RULES OF TURTON F.C., 1873.

## RULES OF THE TURTON FOOTBALL CLUB.

### ESTABLISHED - 1872.

### RULES PUBLISHED 1873.

1.—The choice of Bases is determined by·tossing·

2.—The Bases are twelve feet wide, and the distance between them must not exceed 150 yards. The width of the ground must not be more than 100 yards.

3.—The Ball must be kicked off from the middle of the ground by the side which loses the toss.

4.—The Ball may only be caught (if it has not touched the ground) from a kick by the leg below the knee, or foot; but if, after being kicked, it hits any part of the body of another person before falling to the ground, it may then be caught, except by the kicker·

5.—Whoever catches the ball is entitled to a free kick, if he call " Three Yards "; if he does not call " Three Yards." he is liable to have the Ball knocked out of his hands. N.B.—The Ball must be kicked without delay, and the preliminary run must not be longer than " Three Yards " (that is, the utmost length to which three running strides extend)

6.—The ball when in play, must never be touched by the hand, except in the case of a catch, as above stated.

7.—All charging is fair, but no holding, tripping, pushing with the hands, shinning, or back-shinning is allowed.

8.—If the Ball is kicked beyond the prescribed limits of the ground, it must be kicked straight in again by one of the side opposite to the one who kicked it out. N.B.—When a player is kicking the Ball from behind his own Base, he is not compelled to kick it straight.

9.—If a player catches the Ball near his opponent's Base, he may try to carry the Ball through by taking the " Three Yards." N.B.—No second try is allowed, but in case of a failure, he may still go back and have a free kick.

10.—After a Base has been obtained, or when half-time has elapsed (supposing no Base has been previously obtained), the two sides change their respective bases.

11.—When the Ball is caught, any player on the side of the one making a catch, who is nearer the line of the opponent's base than the catcher, is out of play until the Ball has been touched by one of the opposite side who shall be " behind." Nor must he interfere with one of the opposite side, or in any way prevent or obstruct his catching or kicking the ball.

12.—The Uniform of the Club shall be Blue Knickerbockers, White Stockings, and White Jerseys.

13.—The Ball must pass clearly, in a line between the goal-posts to score a Base.

14.—In case of " Try at Goal," two players shall be chosen, one from each side, to stand behind the kicker. Their decision shall determine whether a goal has been obtained.

The following Rules described as " General Rules " are also interesting :—

1.—There must be two Umpires in each match.

2.—Committee Meetings shall be held the first Tuesday in each month.

## TURTON F.C.

### WINNERS OF JUNIOR SHIELD, 1912-13.

J. Lester (Secretary), N. Fish (Committee), S. Rothwell (Reserve), T. Ward, F. Mellray, J. Farnworth, A. Holt, S. Holt, W. Wallwork (President), D. Roberts (Trainer).

J. Raby, A. Raby, W. Haworth, W. Haworth (junior), T. Knowles.

**M. Bridge, absent from photograph.**

3.—The Committee have power to fix the dates when Members shall meet for play.

4.—The Ball shall not be delivered into any person's possession for play, except that of a Committee man, who is responsible.

5.—The players opposed to the Captain's side shall choose a Captain, and in his absence, each side shall choose a Captain.

6.—All players are under the orders of the Captains during the game.

7.—If the decision of either of the Captains be disputed, the question shall be referred to the Committee.

8.—Each Member intending to leave the Club must send in his resignation to the Secretary, before the commencement of the next season.

9.—An entrance fee of one shilling must be paid on the proposing of a new member.

10.—All Club property must be under the care of the Secretary.

11.—All Subscriptions must be paid to the Treasurer, in advance.

12.—Membership of the " Football Club " includes membership of the " Reading Room," and vice-versa.

**ACCRINGTON F.C.**

WINNERS OF LANCASHIRE CUP, 1880-81.

S. Ormerod, D. Talbot (Captain), J. Lonsdale, W. Latham, J. P. Hartley, J. Yates, J. Riley,
R. Howorth, J. Hindle.
R. Horne, W. J. Whittaker, T. French, W. Eastham.

# CHAPTER IV.

*A. N. Hornby. Petulant and Rebellious Clubs. Blackburn Rovers v. Darwen Dispute. Scene on Alexandra Meadows. J. Lewis attempts to smash the L.F.A. A peculiar Final, 1887-88. Preston North End's refusal to play. Threat to expel Bolton Wanderers. Rishton Club's opinion of the L.F.A. Dr. Morley and his speeches. " Inaccuracy of the Press." Accrington and Preston North End in trouble with The F.A.*

ANYONE who attends the Annual Meetings of the Lancashire F.A. must be struck with not only the quick dispatch of business, but more so with the general cordiality of the meetings, and undoubtedly the strong position that the Association holds, is due to the loyalty of its Clubs.

The present happy experience is in striking contrast to the experience of the Association in its early days, as the following will indicate :—

A. N. Hornby, an honoured name in sport, was the innocent cause of the feud which developed between Blackburn Rovers and Darwen. Mr. Hornby—remembered mostly as a great cricketer and a cricket captain, also as an International Rugby player—was also sufficiently interested in " Soccer " that he turned out for Blackburn Rovers when the latter played their first match v. Patrick on January 2nd, 1878. Mr. Hornby was known as a handy man with the gloves, and at local fairs pitted his science against professional "bruisers." It will therefore be realised that his prowess made him the idol of the Blackburn public. It was very natural that the Rovers should wish to play this attractive personality in a Lancashire Cup Tie v. Darwen in 1880. There was, however, some doubt as to his eligibility, and the point was referred to the Lancashire F.A., who returned the answer " Play him if you wish, and we will consider the matter afterwards," the matter was further complicated and aggravated by the County F.A.

**H. CHIPPENDALE.**
Blackburn Rovers F.C.

**F. BLACKBURN.**
Blackburn Rovers F.C.

**J. HODKINSON.**
Blackburn Rovers F.C.

**JACK SOUTHWORTH.**
Blackburn Rovers F.C.

ordering the Tie to be played at Darwen, which was regarded as another injustice to Blackburn. The Rovers
threatened to refuse to play the Tie, but wiser counsels
prevailed, and the match was played as arranged, though
Mr. Hornby was omitted.

The feeling between Blackburn Rovers and Darwen
was very bitter, and we read the following in the History
of Blackburn Rovers :—

" The ground (Alexandra Meadows) was packed with
spectators, estimated at 10,000, an unusually large number for those days, the Stand was filled, twenty lorries provided extra platform accommodation, and seats were
placed inside the boundary ropes. In the first half the
crowd twice broke through the ropes. The score was 1-1
at half-time. In the second period play had been in progress eight minutes when Marshall (Darwen), on being
robbed of the ball by Suter (Rovers), seized the Blackburn
player in his arms and threw him down near the spectators.
The crowd promptly invaded the field . . . . and the
match had to be abandoned. A gentleman present at the
match told the writer that his impression was that the
spectators temporarily lost their heads, in consequence of
the dispute between the two players, and the position was
aggravated by the extreme rivalry of the Clubs. Whatever
the correct version may be, the fact remains that the hatchet
was not buried until the beginning of 1882."

In the meantime disputes between Blackburn Rovers
and Darwen were frequent. One of them related to a
Lancashire Cup Tie, and the L.F.A. took the exceptional
and severe course of expelling both Clubs from the Lancashire Cup Competition. The Rovers retaliated by inducing
celebrated Scotch teams to visit them on dates fixed for
Lancashire Cup Ties. The County Cup Final between
Accrington and Park Road, played at Darwen, only attracted the small " gate " of £51 17s. 3d., whereas the Rovers'
friendly matches were better patronised.

The late John Lewis severed his connection with the
L.F.A. and he set out to smash the organisation of which
he was a founder. The Lancashire F.A. suffered severely

financially, and they were beset with difficulties, and had recourse to seek the help of The F.A.

The following extract from the Football Annual of 1881 is of interest :—

" The Committee of the Lancashire Association were placed in a most difficult position in consequence of the disinclination of the Blackburn Rovers and Darwen to act in concert with them, and as a rule the teams which did battle for the County were in no way representative. The Season was opened auspiciously with victories over Staffordshire and North Wales, but reverses attended them in all their subsequent engagements, and the unsportsmanlike behaviour of the Blackburn Rovers produced a rupture which might have endangered the very existence of the Association. But the greatest credit was due to the Committee for their resolute action, which met with the unanimous approval of the Conference at Manchester, and it is satisfactory to note that the misunderstanding was finally healed, and the Rovers re-instated in the Lancashire Association· The subject is a painful one, but it would be shirking a duty were I to refrain from stating that the conduct of those who had management of affairs on behalf of the Rovers was anything but creditable·

The unseemly disturbance in a club match between Darwen and Blackburn Rovers, on the ground of the latter, culminated in so much ill-feeling between these Clubs that they would not arrange to play their tie for the Lancashire Cup, and their subsequent conduct, which resulted in the removal of both from the later ties, showed what an unwholesome prominence the ' gate ' occupies in the consideration of football clubs in the North. Indeed, there is no use to disguise the speedy approach of a time when the subject of professional players will require the earnest attention of those on whom devolves the management of Association football."

Another peculiar incident occurred in Season 1887-8, and the offending Club on this occasion was Preston North End. This dispute also arose from the arrangements made for the Lancashire Cup Final Tie. The finalists were

## BLACKBURN OLYMPIC F.C.
WINNERS OF THE F.A. CUP, 1882-1883.

W. Bramham (Secretary), G. Wilson, T. Dewhurst, T. Hacking, J. T. Ward,
A. Astley (Treasurer).
J. Costley, J. Hunter, J. Yates, W. Astley.
T. Gibson, A. Warburton (Captain), A. Matthews.

Accrington and Preston North End, and the match  was
fixed to be played at Blackburn, and though North End
flatly refused to play there, the L.F.A. were determined to
proceed with their arrangements.  The Final Tie, Accrington v. North End, was therefore duly advertised, but  the
Witton Club was also arranged with, and paid the sum of
£10 0s. 0d. to be in readiness to play a match with Accrington in the event of North End failing to turn up.  Preston
North End did not turn up, and therefore Witton  played
Accrington, and actually beat them by four goals to none.
The late Mr. C. Crump was the Referee.  The " gate "
receipts were £43 15s. 8d., and the match expenses £38
14s. 0d.  It will therefore be seen that the L.F.A. were
financially hardly pressed.

It stands as a peculiar record that Accrington F.C. won
the Lancashire Cup in 1887-8, though defeated in the Final
by Witton F.C., whom Accrington had already beaten 2-1
in the Semi-Final Tie.  The refusal of North End to turn
out in the Final Tie had left a set of " Runners up " medals
in hand, and it was decided that the two Clubs who had
been beaten in the Semi-Final Ties should play off for them.
Witton and Darwen Old Wanderers therefore played at
Darwen, and Witton won by two goals to nil, the " gate "
receipts being £11 12s. 2d., and the expenses £9 1s. 2d.
This period was a black one for the L.F.A., who certainly
" touched the bottom."

Since the Great War there has been no more loyal and
helpful Member of the Association than Bolton Wanderers,
who have greatly assisted the work of the Association by
taking a keen interest in the Lancashire Cup Competition,
and in allowing the Association the use of Burnden Park
for many of its Finals and for Amateur County Matches,
yet it was touch and go in November, 1883, whether the
Wanderers should be expelled from the Association.  Indeed, The F.A. recommended that the Club should be expelled because the Referee, the late Mr. Sam Ormerod,
was " hooted on the field," " that he was followed from
the Pikes Lane ground by a crowd, that he was assaulted,
and that the Club did not take steps for his protection on

the way to the Station." Fortunately, the L.F.A. decided, rightly or wrongly, " that no further action should be taken as no good could result therefrom." If The F.A.'s recommendation had been carried out, Lancashire would have lost a Club which has since risen to the greatest heights of fame.

Not only were Clubs difficult to manage, but there were individuals who caused the Members of the L.F.A. to think furiously. So far back as January, 1882, there was a postcard from Rishton F.C. as follows:—" Will you please appoint a Referee for our match with Bolton Wanderers on Saturday, at Bolton. We would rather not have a Member of the Lancashire F.A., they are so one sided." The following story of a dispute with the late Dr. Morley may show that the Association was then " one sided," or it may show that there was " another side."

Dr. Morley, brother of the late Viscount Morley, of Blackburn, was a stormy petrel. He was a man of pugnacious temperament and of strong convictions. The Doctor was a Vice-President of Blackburn Rovers, and from 1882-84 he was also a Vice-President of the Lancashire F.A. It was during the latter period that we read that " Mr. T. Hindle reported to the L.F.A. Committee, who met at Darwen on 13th September, 1883, that Dr. Morley (who was present at the meeting) had used the following words in a speech at the Annual Meeting of the Rovers F.C. :—

" He (Dr. Morley) wished to express his strong disapprobation of the conduct of the L.F.A. Committee. He then referred to the Dinners that had been provided for the winners of the Lancashire Cup the two previous years, adding that this year they—the Association—had come to that conclusion, because they were the Blackburn Rovers they were not to have a Dinner." He (Dr. Morley) protested against that, and that was what he wanted to slap the Lancashire F.A. in the face for, " There was nothing they (the Rovers) could do, the Association did not readily take advantage of." The Minutes merely inform us that the Committee " considered the remarks of the Doctor contrary to the interests of the Association," and that Dr. Morley stated that " he was not correctly reported," the Committee decided that " Dr. Morley be respectfully requested to contradict the report," and at a further meeting a letter was read from the Doctor threatening to resign his position as a Vice-President, and the Committee decided to ask him to re-consider his decision. The matter was not however allowed to rest, and at a further Committee Meeting it was decided " to call a General Meeting of the Association to consider the language used by Dr. Morley, and to take such steps as may be deemed fit and proper." The Special General Meeting was held in Blackburn on 18th November, 1883, at which there was a large attendance of Clubs. Dr. Morley again blamed the Press for inaccurately reporting him, and finally the Meeting passed a resolution, " regretting that the Doctor did not contradict the inaccurate statements complained of."

In passing, it may be of interest to know that it is recorded that the Annual Meeting held in 1884 " lasted three hours and a half, and then broke up."

In December, 1883, the Accrington F.C. had evidently been giving trouble to The F.A., for we read, "The following Resolution respecting the reported expulsion of the Accrington F.C. from The Football Association was passed, and Mr. T. Hindle was appointed to attend the Meeting of The F.A., and lay the views of this Association before that Meeting. Resolved that this Committee after carefully considering the Resolution passed by The F.A. expelling the Accrington Club, is strongly of opinion that a Club can only be expelled by a special General Meeting called for the purpose."

In January, 1884, the L.F.A. took up the cudgels on behalf of Preston North End, who had been struck out of The F.A. Cup Competition.

We have referred to the above distasteful squabbles as matters of history, but rejoice to know that loyalty and good sense smoothed over the troubles, and we believe the Clubs are now happy in their relationship towards each other and the County F.A.

LANCASHIRE F.A. COUNCIL AT BOLTON ABBEY. 1907.

Standing: T. Y. Ritson, T. Houghton, H. Hamer (Hon. Auditor), J. T. Howcroft (Referees' Registrar), E. Little, R. Birtwistle, J. J. Haworth, J. Cooper, R. P. Gregson, W. Gilgryst, A. H. Downs (Hon. Auditor), C. E. Sutcliffe.
Seated: T. Duxbury, W. A. Duckworth, J. J. Bentley, W. E. Ord. J. S. Roscow, J. Lewis, R. Watson.

D

# CHAPTER V.—AN EVERTON CHAPTER.

*Everton's application to play in the Lancashire Cup Competition declined. When admitted the Club endeavours to play " mixed " teams, wishes to " scratch," withdraws from the Competition. Everton again apply to play for the Lancashire Cup. Everton fined £25 also £100 for playing " weak " Teams, the Club appeals to The F.A. A keen dispute.*

WHEN it is stated that Everton unsuccessfully applied to be included in the Lancashire Cup Competition there is no joke intended, the statement is true even though it be curious.

The minutes of the Association for 5th August, 1886, contain the following record :—

Resolved—'' That Everton be not allowed to play for the Senior Cup until they show proof of their ability,'' and therefore the Club stayed in the Junior Cup Competition and played Fleetwood Zingari. However, on 6th September, 1887, we read '' The application by Everton F.C. to play in the Senior Cup Competition be granted,'' but the club's experience was not altogether a happy one for a long time.

In November, 1897, Everton applied to play a '' mixed '' team or to '' scratch,'' but permission was refused, the following year there was a further application to '' scratch '' which was again refused. So far back as 1893 the club had trouble with the Association in connection with a Senior Cup Tie with Blackburn Rovers, and in 1896 the Club must have been evading the Competition rules in some way, because it is recorded that the Club be written to for an explanation, no details are given, and a little later we read '' The reply from the Everton F.C. is not satisfactory.''

In 1898 Everton withdrew from the Lancashire Competition, but applied for re-admission the following year after the Association had passed a resolution '' That the Lancashire F.A. consider playing Lancashire Cup Ties on week days, other than Saturdays.''

It was thought that the playing of the Cup Ties on

Mondays would bring peace where there had been unrest and rebellion, but such was not the case, indeed, it was evident that clubs played " weak " teams, and the Secretary was instructed on 4th October, 1905, to " write all the clubs who do not play their full strength," and this policy brought about a most remarkable state of affairs, the Association being determined to keep faith with the public, in securing the proper playing of the matches, or to deal with the offending clubs.

One of the keenest fights waged against the Lancashire F.A. was made by Everton F.C in 1908-09. The matter arose out of the Club's disinclination to play its " full strength " in the Senior Cup Competition. It should be recalled that up to 1899 Lancashire Cup Ties were played on Saturdays, then came the power and influence of The Football League Clubs, and they petitioned for the matches to be played in Mid-Week, and that change was made for Season 1899-1900. For a time the matches were well attended and well played, but eventually it became apparent that certain Clubs were breaking and evading the Cup Rules. Everton F.C. was evidently regarded as one of the guilty Clubs, for a fine of £25/0/0 was imposed on the 4th November, 1908, because of weak teams played v. Burnley in the 2nd Round and v. Blackpool in the 3rd Round; but the real tug-of-war commenced when the Semi-Final Ties were played on the 23rd November, 1908, Everton being drawn to play Liverpool at Goodison Park.

On the previous Saturday Everton had played the following team in a League Match v. Blackburn Rovers :—

Scott; Balmer, Macconachie; Harris, Taylor, Make-peace; Sharp, Coleman, Freeman, Young, Geo. Barlow.

But on the following Monday when they were required to play their " full strength," the following team stepped on the field :—

Bury; Strettle, Balmer; Rafferty, Borthwick, Adamson; Buck, Coleman, Jones, Young, Dawson.

Incidentally the team for the 28th November was identical with that which played on 21st November. Before the kick-off and during the Cup Tie played on 23rd

November, Officials of Everton F.C. were full of excuses for
the weak team on the field, and an assurance was made
and often repeated " that all the players would be triers."
A request was also made that the regular players, who were
not playing because of alleged sickness and injuries should
be inspected. Mr. R. Watson, a Member of the L.F.A., who
was present, was invited to view the sick and lame, but he
adroitly refused on the grounds that he was present as a
Linesman of the match, and that the inspection of injured
players was outside his duties.    Mr. E. Little, then a
Divisional Member of the L.F.A., and now a Vice-President, was also present at the match, but he also was not
anxious to accept the commission, and he declined on the
grounds " that he was not a medical man."    Mr. F. Hargreaves who was present on behalf of the then Secretary,
" Dick " Gregson, also refused the invitation to inspect the
cripples, but suggested that medical certificates should be
sent to the Association.   The game was a poor one, and
Everton lost by two goals to none.   The Everton
F.C. sent medical certificates referring to certain players,
and the matter was reviewed by the Council at a meeting
held on 2nd December, 1908, when it was decided to fine
the Club the sum of £100, and also to fine them the amount
due to them as their share of the "gate" receipts, £99/0/9.
The Everton F.C. then began a vigorous protest, and
eventually the Council decided to call a Special Meeting
to re-consider the case.   The meeting was held on 6th
January, 1909, when it was decided to adhere to the fines
imposed.

The following day, Mr. W. C. Cuff, who was then
Secretary of Everton F.C., lodged an appeal with The F.A.
which was heard on 2nd April, 1909.   The late John Lewis
stated the case for Lancashire F.A., and Mr. W. C. Cuff
for Everton F.C., and the decision of The F.A. was to
reduce the fine to £100, which implied that the definite fine
imposed was quite in order, whereas the resolution to de-
prive the Everton Club of its share of the " gate " receipts
was not in order, and so ended the only appeal by any
Club against the Association.

THE LANCASHIRE CUP.

# CHAPTER VI.—LANCASHIRE CUP COMPETITION.

*The First Final Tie. The First Draw. The Cup won on 46
occasions. Records of winning clubs. " Gate " Receipts,
Pre-War and Post-War. Mr. Sutcliffe's 1919 Scheme.
Revival of Interest. Extraordinary figures. Remarkable
scene at Oldham. The Competition vital to Lancashire F.A.*

———— —

The Lancashire Cup was first competed for in Season
1879-80. Darwen F.C. were the first winners. The match
was played at Darwen, the teams being Darwen v. Blackburn Rovers. Darwen won by three goals to none. The
" gate " receipts were £167, and 9,000 spectators were
present.

Forms from Schools were borrowed, and these were
placed on lorries, the latter also borrowed, and those con-
stituted the " Grand Stand." Such arrangements are interesting when one compares them with the gigantic structures,
complete with every convenience and comfort, now to be
found on so many grounds.

The First Draw, which therefore shews the original Cup
Clubs, was as follows :—

*Made 16th August, 1879, at the Coffee Tavern,
Darwen Street, Blackburn.*

| | |
|---|---|
| North End (Bolton) | v Turton. |
| Padiham | v. Haslingden. |
| Astley Bridge | v. Rising Sun (Blackburn). |
| Accrington | v. Halliwell. |
| St. Paul's (Bolton) | v. St. Mark's (Blackburn). |
| Lower Darwen | v. Darwen Rangers. |
| Bolton Olympic | v. Lynwood (Darwen). |
| Darwen St. James | v. Haslingden Grane. |

| | |
|---|---|
| Middleton | v. Edgeworth. |
| Cloughfold | v. Great Lever. |
| Darwen Grasshoppers | v. Darwen. |
| Cob Wall | v. Manchester Wanderers. |
| Livesey United (Blackburn) | v. Halliwell Jubilee. |
| Bolton Hornets | v. Blackburn Christ Church |
| Enfield | v. Blackburn Rovers. |
| Bolton Wanderers | v. All Saints (Bolton). |
| Blackburn St. George's | v. Lower Chapel (Darwen) |
| Bolton Rovers. | v. Eagley |
| Church | v. Blackburn St. Andrews |
| Blackburn Park Road | v. Emmanuel (Bolton). |

The Cup has been won 46 times, as follows :—

Accrington—Three times, 1880-81, 1887-88, 1888-89.

Blackburn Rovers—Eleven times, 1881-82, 1882-83, 1883-84, 1884-85, 1895-96, 1900-01, 1901-02, 1903-04, 1906-07, 1908-09, 1910-11.

Bolton Wanderers—Six times, 1885-86, 1890-91, 1911-12, 1921-22, 1924-25, 1926-27.

Burnley—Twice, 1889-90, 1914-15.

Bury—Five times, 1891-92, 1898-99, 1902-03, 1905-06, 1925-26.

Darwen—Once, 1879-80.

Everton—Three times, 1893-94, 1896-97, 1909-10.

Liverpool—Twice, 1918-19, 1923-24, and in 1919-20, they held it jointly with Manchester United.

Manchester United—Three times, 1897-98, 1912-13, 1913-14, and in 1919-20, they held it jointly with Liverpool.

Manchester City—Three times, 1920-21, 1922-23, 1927-28.

Oldham Athletic—Once, 1907-08.

Preston North End—Four times, 1886-87, 1892-93, 1894-95, 1899-1900.

Southport—Once, 1904-05.

The Trophy which cost £160, and is one of the finest
Cups in the Country, was not played for in the following
Seasons during the Great War, 1915-16, 1916-17, 1917-18.

In 1900-01 Blackburn Rovers and Bury played each
other in five matches, actually playing eight hours and 26
minutes before the issue was decided, the scores being
0—0, 0—0, 3—3, 1—1, and finally 3—1 for the Rovers.

Largest scores in Semi-Final and Final Ties :—

1886-87 Semi-Final—Preston North End 12, Witton 0.
At Bolton.

1892-93 Semi-Final—Preston North End 6, Bootle 4.
At Liverpool.

1908-09 Semi-Final—Blackburn Rovers 7, Manchester
City 0.  At Blackburn.

1908-09 Final—Blackburn Rovers 5, Liverpool 3.  At
Blackburn.

1910-11  Semi-Final—Everton 6, Blackburn Rovers 1.
At Everton.

1912-13 Semi-Final, Blackburn Rovers 6, Manchester
City 1.  At Blackburn.

1925-26 Final—Bury 5, Accrington Stanley 3.  At
Bolton.

In 1926 Manchester City beat Oldham Athletic 8 goals
to 4 at Maine Road in the Second Round, and in 1910-11
Blackburn Rovers and Burnley met four times in the Final
Tie, the matches resulting :—

Rovers 1,   Burnley 1.  At Ewood Park.
Rovers 2,   Burnley 2.  At Turf Moor.
Rovers 0,   Burnley 0.  At Burnden Park.
Rovers 2,   Burnley 1.  At Ewood Park.

Other large scores were :—

Season 1884-5  Blackburn Olympic 18, Leigh 0.
               Darwen Old Wanderers 17, Scout Bottom
                   Blue Ribbon 2.
               Lower Darwen 15, Springhill (Burnley) 0.
               Bolton Wanderers 10, Hurst Park Road 2.

Season 1882-3  Bolton Wanderers 10, Rishton 1.  (After a draw 2—2).

Season 1886-7  Bolton Wanderers 14; Wigan 0.

There have been the following large " gate " receipts :

## PRE-WAR.

1886-1887.  Final Tie.  Preston North End v. Bolton Wanderers.  At Bolton.  £335/11/3.

1890-91.  Semi-Final Tie.  Bolton Wanderers v. Blackburn Rovers.  At Ardwick.  £484/18/6.

1894-95.  Semi-Final Tie.  Everton v. Liverpool.  At Everton.  £739/10/10.

1896-97.  Semi-Final Tie.  Everton v. Burnley.  At Everton.  £544/18/9.

1896-97.  Semi-Final Tie.  Manchester City v. Bolton Wanderers.  At Manchester.  £341/12/0.

1911-12.  Final Tie.  Bolton Wanderers v. Burnley.  At Bolton.  £371/6/9.

## POST-WAR.

1919-20.  Final Tie.  Manchester United v. Liverpool. At Liverpool.  £1081/4/8.

1920-21.  Final Tie.  Manchester City v. Bolton Wanderers.  At Old Trafford.  £1,640/11/0.

1921-22.  Final Tie.  Bury v. Bolton Wanderers. At Bury.  £1,018/17/9.

1924-25.  Final Tie.  Bolton Wanderers v Blackpool. At Bolton.  £794/2/6.

1927-28.  Final Tie.  Bury v. Manchester City. At Old Trafford.  £1,365/10/0.

The least " gate " in a Final Tie was when Blackburn Rovers played Southport at Deepdale, the Receipts being only £51/15/9.

Just prior to the Great War the interest in the Competition was very limited, but since the War the Competition has been most interesting, attractive, and a financial success.

When the Competition was resumed, thanks to Mr. C. E. Sutcliffe, who formulated a scheme whereby the Clubs playing in the Lancahire Section of The Football League (a War time arrangement) should compete for the Lancashire Cup under the following conditions.

The Clubs were divided into the following groups :—

| Group 1. | Group 2. |
|---|---|
| Manchester City. | Everton. |
| Manchester United. | Liverpool. |
| Stoke | Southport. |
| Port Vale. | Stockport County. |

| Group 3. | Group 4. |
|---|---|
| Bolton Wanderers. | Blackburn Rovers. |
| Bury. | Blackpool. |
| Oldham Athletic. | Burnley. |
| Rochdale. | Preston North End |

The results of the matches played under The Football League to determine the winner of each group, and the four winners were the Semi-Finalists of the Cup Competition, and the following Clubs qualified :—Manchester City, Liverpool, Oldham Athletic, and Blackpool.

The Semi-Final Ties were :—

Blackpool v. Liverpool.  Gross " gate " £404.

Manchester City v. Oldham Athletic (At Hyde Road). Gross " gate " £1,193.

(Replay at Oldham).  Gross " gate " £1,090.

Final Tie.  Liverpool v. Oldham Athletic.  (At Old Trafford).  Gross " gate " £1,305.

**BURNLEY F.C.**

WINNERS OF LANCASHIRE CUP, 1889-90.

W. McFeteridge, W. Bury, J. Kearsley (Umpire), D. Speirs, E. T. White (Secretary).
J. Haresnape, A. McLardie, A. Lang, C. Lambie, A. Stewart, J. Hill.
A. Kay, J. Keenan.

These were extraordinary figures and resulted in a nett sum of £3,200 accruing to the Association. Such a success established the Lancashire F.A. in a sound financial position, and made possible all the help that has since been given to juvenile, minor, amateur, and junior football.

Most remarkable scenes were witnessed at Oldham in May, 1919, on the occasion of the Semi-Final Tie, Re-play, Oldham Athletic and Manchester City.

As the late Mr. J. Lewis, then President of the L.F.A., and Mr. F. Hargreaves, Secretary, were walking down Sheepfoot Lane towards Boundary Park, they saw with great satisfaction many hundreds of people crowding round the entrances, and were just remarking upon the animated scene, when the crowds referred to disappeared like magic, a large door having been forced open and some of the hoardings pulled down.

Mr. Lewis dashed to the scene in great haste, the Secretary having failed to convince him that nothing could be done, and when Mr. Hargreaves arrived at the place of the " break in," he found the late President in trouble with the Police, Mr. Lewis had attempted to follow through where hundreds of people had gained free admission, his object being to discover the cause of the happening and the approximate number who had rushed through, but by this time the Police had taken control, and as Mr. Lewis was entering the ground he was unceremoniously turned back, he insisted that he had a right to enter the ground, but the Police Officer—who did not know him—was adamant. The position was becoming threatening when the L.F.A. Secretary strolled up, took in the situation, presented his official card to the Inspector, and also at that moment " Latic " officials came on the scene and peace was restored.

The Lancashire Cup Competition is necessary to maintain the work of the Lancashire Football Association, nurturing minor and juvenile football, assisting junior football, and in the comprehensive work of sanctioning and controlling all classes of football within the County.

The Association takes 20 per cent. of the nett " gate " receipts of all matches prior to the Semi-Final Ties, and takes one third of the nett " gate " receipts in the Semi-Final Ties and the Final Tie. Handsome gold medals, of equal value, are given to the Winners and Runners-up.

Since the Great War, the Competition has been exclusively confined to the Clubs playing in The Football League, and it is again played for on the knock-out principle. It can be confidently claimed that the Competition has been a success since the War, both from a playing and also a " paying " point of view.

The success of the Competition is vital to the work of the Association, and therefore to football generally.

Often one has heard the remark, " it is only a Lancashire Cup Tie," yet some of the finest football has often been witnessed in these games.

# CHAPTER VII.—OUR PRESIDENT.

## CHARLES E. SUTCLIFFE.

A Solicitor by profession.

Elected a member of the Lancashire F.A. Council in 1896, was due to receive his Long Service Medal in 1917, but that was deferred until 1918 because of the Great War. He was elected a Vice-President of the Association in 1918, and was Deputy-President of the Association when Mr. J. Lewis went to Australia with The F.A. Team in 1925.

Mr. Sutcliffe was elected President on 21st January, 1926, he is Chairman of the Finance and Rules Revision Committees, and an ex-officio member of all other committes.

He represents Lancashire on the Council of The F.A., and there serves on the following Committees :—

International Selection Committee.
Referees' Committee and
Rules Revision Committee.

Mr. Sutcliffe is a Vice-President of The Football League, to which he was first elected in 1898, he is a member of the International League Board and of the Anglo-Irish League Board, also President of the Northern Counties Amateur Championship and serves on the Appeals Committees of about twenty Leagues.

---

The above is only a bare indication of the many offices held by the President of the Lancashire F.A., and how he, in addition to being engaged in a large legal practice, can find time to devote to all the football matches. meetings, functions, etc., is a mystery to his closest friends.

Mr. Sutcliffe has been described as the '' brains of Football,'' and '' R.G.,'' of the '' Sporting Chronicle,'' once aptly named him the '' Foch of Football.''

**C. E. SUTCLIFFE.**

President, Lancashire F.A.   Elected January 21st, 1926.
Vice-President, The Football League,
and
Member of The Football Association Council.

Mr. Sutcliffe in an interview with " R.G." in 1918 disclosed the secret that had it not been for the Great War, his association with football would by then have been ended.

Why Mr. Sutcliffe had arrived at that decision is not known, but I can surmise that the War having shaken football organisations to their very foundations, that Mr. Sutcliffe—whatever his previous intentions—felt that he must continue to take his part, helping to re-establish and re-organise the game.

Mr. Sutcliffe was born at Burnley, and has played both Soccer and Rugby.

The last match that Mr. Sutcliffe played in was against Blackburn Rovers on the old Leamington ground, and as left-half back he was pitted against Joe Lofthouse the famous international, the Burnley captain gave Mr. Sutcliffe strict orders to watch Lofthouse, and he did, but in his own words he confessed " but it was months before I got rid of the bruises I collected. I shall never forget it. I am not suggesting that Lofthouse was unfair. I had nothing to complain of, but the top and bottom of it was, I could not stop him." Mr. Sutcliffe was one of the first members of the International League Board, and drafted the first Rules. He was elected a Director of Burnley F.C. when the club was made into a limited liability company.

It was Mr. Sutcliffe who moved the abolition of the Test matches.

Mr. Sutcliffe is in his 30th year as a member of The Football League, and for many years he has not only revised and selected the referees and linesmen and made the draft appointments, but has also made the fixtures of The Football League and the Central League.

Prior to becoming a legislator, Mr. Sutcliffe was a referee for several years, he was a Football League Referee and for four successive years he officiated in every International match in which England did not take part.

E

Like all other referees, Mr. Sutcliffe had his " experiences," it even being alleged that in a memorable match
Sunderland  v.  Small  Heath  (now  Birmingham)  he
" escaped " from the ground dressed as a policeman.

In September, 1896, Mr. Sutcliffe refereed the League
match Rovers v. Liverpool at Ewood Park, and had the
temerity to disallow six goals.      Later in the game the
Rovers scored a good goal which won the match.

Mr. Sutcliffe was one of the founders of the Referees'
Union, and was its first President, and when he resigned in
1913 he was presented with a gold watch.

Along with Mr. T. H Sidney, of Wolverhampton, Mr.
Sutcliffe took up the case of The Football League v. The
Football Association with reference to the " retain and
transfer system " of professionals, with the result that The
F.A. changed its attitude on that matter.

Mr. Sutcliffe also professionally represented The
Football League in the action H. C. Kingaby v. Aston Villa,
which case established the legality of the retain and transfer
system,  he also represented Mr. P. Kelso, Manager of
Fulham F.C. in the action brought against him by Mr. F. A.
Charrington for an assault alleged to have been committed
on the Fulham ground when Mr. Charrington was decrying
wartime football.

Mr. Sutcliffe was also engaged in the famous West
Trials which took place at the Royal Courts of Justice in
1917 and 1918, arising from the " squared " match between
Manchester United and Liverpool, played at Manchester on
Good Friday of 1915.

Space will not allow us to dwell on the travelling ex-
ploits of The President. When he is not rushing midnight or
early morning to London, Birmingham or Scotland by rail,
he is either in his office or speeding by road to Court work
or in attendance at L.F.A. meetings.

During Season 1926-27 Mr. Sutcliffe actually attended
all possible (58) meetings of the Lancashire F.A. in addition

### J. McKENNA.

President of The Football League,
Vice-President of The Football Association and
Vice-President of Lancashire F.A.

to which there were many interviews and consultations with the Association Secretary, various Dinners, Cup Presentations, etc.

During the War the Lancashire F.A. lost many of its valued leaders, and the resumption of the game in 1919 saw Mr. John Lewis in command as President. It is no secret that the successful work of reconstruction was initiated, guided and developed by the present President. It was during that period that Mr. Sutcliffe formulated an emergency Lancashire Cup Competition, which was so successful that it not merely gave back to the Association all that had been lost during the War period, but it gave the Association the greatest balance it had ever had, so much so, that five years afterwards the Shylocks of Income Tax Authorities demanded their pound of flesh, and got it.

The possession of ample funds enabled the Association to not only buy its own premises, but also to give that necessary assistance to all classes of football which previously it had not been able to help.

When Mr. J. Lewis was suddenly called to join the " great majority " in January of 1926, the members of the L.F.A. Council unanimously elected Mr. Sutcliffe President of the Association. No other man was thought of, even though there were others with longer years of service.

The Association has grown enormously in its membership, in its comprehensive work, in its activities for School boy, Minor, Junior, Intermediate and Senior Football. The increased work and changed conditions demanded—and still demands—a man of courage, daring, long experience, breadth of view, tactful and tolerant, not merely to be the President, but to act as leader, chairman, guide, counsellor and friend, and the occasion found the man—fitted—gifted—and willing to serve.

The destinies of the Association are safe in the hands of Our President, Charles E. Sutcliffe.

# CHAPTER VIII.—THE FOOTBALL LEAGUE.

If we were writing a full history of football the Competition provided by The Football League would form an important part, for it is the greatest competition in the game. Formed on 17th April, 1888, The Football League at first consisted of 12 Clubs of which Accrington, Blackburn Rovers, Bolton Wanderers, Burnley, Everton and Preston North End were in membership. At the time this record was penned, Blackburn Rovers, Burnley, Bury, Everton, Liverpool and Manchester United are in the First Division, Blackpool, *Manchester City, Oldham Athletic and Preston North End in the Second, and Accrington Stanley, Barrow, Nelson, Rochdale, Southport and Wigan Borough in the Third.

The Football League was formed at Manchester after a preliminary Meeting in London, and has throughout its existence had a large Lancashire flavour—both in its composition, government, and the spirit with which it was conducted. For the first 3 seasons the League comprised 12 Clubs, but in season 1891-92, 2 Clubs were added, and in 1892-93 another 2. The constitution remained at 16 until 1898-99, when the Clubs were increased to 18, and the further increases were to 20 for season 1905-06, and to 22 when League football was resumed after the war for season 1919-20. The latest increase was due to the memorable " squared game," and allowed Chelsea to be re-elected, good fortune also falling the way of The Arsenal Club.

At the end of season 1897-98 The Football League scrapped the test matches. Mr. C. E. Sutcliffe proposed

---

* Manchester City won promotion to Division I. in May, 1928.

the abolition, and the League substituted the principle of promotion and relegation.

The Second Division was formed in 1892-93 with 12 Clubs, increased to 15 the following season, to 16 in 1894-95, to 18 in 1898-99, after which increases were made as in the First Division.

The Third Division (Southern Section), commenced operations in 1920-21 with 22 Clubs, but the Northern Section was not included until the following season, starting with 20 Clubs and increased to 22 for season 1923-24. The Football League now practically covers England and Wales from North to South and East to West. Providing as it does a full season's Competition it is the financial backbone of the Clubs. The Lancashire Clubs have kept pace with the growth of the game in a way that few Counties can boast of. All the First and Second Division Clubs grounds have been rebuilt, with the result that most of them have found favour for representative games. Records have been set up at various grounds, notably Everton, Manchester United, and Burnley, for the latter Club provided a record for The Football League Inter-League game, and for attendance at a Football Association trial game. Blackpool is the favoured resort for the Amateurs, and their enterprise is sure to command further honours.

In the Managerial side of The League there have only been 3 Presidents, the late Mr. W. McGregor, the late Mr. J. J. Bentley and Mr. J. McKenna. Amongst the early members of the Management Committee were Mr. R. Molyneux (Everton) and Mr. J. Parlby (Manchester City). The late Mr. J. Lewis received a League long service medal, and Dr. Baxter (Everton) was a member of the Committee of Management for several years. Mr. C. E. Sutcliffe is the senior member of the Management Committee and a Vice-President, whilst Mr. T. A. Barcroft and Mr. W. C. Cuff have joined the Committee more recently. The long record of Mr. McKenna and Mr. Sutcliffe testify to the assistance Lancashire has given to The Football League. It is only necessary to add that Mr. T. Charnley, the Secretary, who has acted as such for twenty-six years, is a Lancashire man, and the Offices of The League are situate at Preston in Lancashire.

---

## LANCASHIRE CLUBS WHO HAVE WON THE FOOTBALL LEAGUE CHAMPIONSHIPS.

| DIVISION 1. | | DIVISION 2. | |
|---|---|---|---|
| 1888-89. | Preston North End. | 1893-94. | Liverpool. |
| 1889-90. | Preston North End. | 1894-95. | Bury. |
| 1890-91. | Everton. | 1895-96. | Liverpool. |
| 1900-01. | Liverpool. | 1897-98. | Burnley. |
| 1905-06. | Liverpool. | 1898-99. | Manchester City. |
| 1907-08. | Manchester United | 1902-03. | Manchester City. |
| 1910-11. | Manchester United | 1903-04. | Preston North End. |
| 1911-12. | Blackburn Rovers. | 1904-05. | Liverpool. |
| 1913-14. | Blackburn Rovers. | 1908-09. | Bolton Wanderers. |
| 1914-15. | Everton. | 1909-10. | Manchester City. |
| 1920-21. | Burnley. | 1912-13. | Preston North End |
| 1921-22. | Liverpool. | 1927-28. | Manchester City. |
| 1922-23. | Liverpool. | | |
| 1927-28. | Everton. | | |

UNIQUE COLLECTION OF FAMOUS TROPHIES.

LANCASHIRE CUP FINAL TIE, 12th MAY, 1928. MANCHESTER CITY, 3 GOALS; BURY, 1 GOAL.

T. Laithwaite, Hon. Treasurer, Lancashire F.A.; W. J. Sawyer, Director Everton F.C., and L.F.A. Member; R. Crompton. Director Blackburn Rovers F.C.; F. Hargreaves, Secretary Lancashire F.A.; L. Furniss, Chairman Manchester City F.C.; H. Duckworth, Chairman Bury F.C., and L.F.A. Member; C. E. Sutcliffe, President Lancashire F.A.; C. E. Foweraker, Secretary Bolton Wanderers F.C., and L.F.A. Member.

The Football League Championship Cup, First Division.    The F.A. Cup.    The Football League Championship Shield, Second Division.    The Lancashire Cup.

[PHOTO BY ALLIED PRESS, LTD.]

.

The following Lancashire Clubs have won The F.A.
Cup : —

1882-83.  Blackburn Olympic beat Old Etonians 2—1,
after an extra half-hour at the Oval.

1883-84.  Blackburn Rovers beat Queen's Park (Glasgow)
2—1 at the Oval.

1884-85.  Blackburn Rovers beat Queen's Park (Glasgow)
2—0 at the Oval.

1885-86.  Blackburn Rovers beat West Bromwich Albion
2—0 at Derby, after a draw 0—0 at the Oval.

1888-89.  Preston North End beat Wolverhampton
Wanderers 3—0 at the Oval.

1889-90.  Blackburn Rovers beat Sheffield Wednesday
6—1 at the Oval.

1890-91.  Blackburn Rovers beat Notts County 3—1 at
the Oval.

1899-1900. Bury beat Southampton 4—0 at the Crystal
Palace.

1902-03.  Bury beat Derby County 6—0 at the Crystal
Palace.

1903-04.  Manchester City beat Bolton Wanderers 1—0
at Crystal Palace.

1905-06.  Everton beat Newcastle United 1—0 at the
Crystal Palace.

1908-09.  Manchester United beat Bristol City 1—0 at
the Crystal Palace.

1913-14.  Burnley beat Liverpool 1—0 at the Crystal
Palace.

1922-23.  Bolton Wanderers beat West Ham United 2—0
at Wembley.

1925-26.  Bolton Wanderers beat Manchester City 1—0
at Wembley.

1927-28.  Blackburn Rovers beat Huddersfield Town
3—1 at Wembley.

THE LANCASHIRE JUNIOR CUP.

# CHAPTER IX.—THE JUNIOR CUP.

*Its inception. Bell's Temperance First Winners. Table Rappings. Turton's Record. Other Winners. Lancaster Town's remarkable experiences. Skerton records. "Gate" Receipts. Rivalry of non-Lancashire Combination Clubs to defeat their " peers."*

## LANCASHIRE FOOTBALL ASSOCIATION.
## JUNIOR CUP COMPETITION.

THIS Competition was established in 1885, because of the rapid growth of the game at that period, and also because the entries for the Lancashire Cup (Senior) Competition were so very numerous.

To use a very common expression the Junior Cup Competition "caught on," no doubt many Clubs felt that at any rate they had a reasonable chance of success, whereas previously they were pitted against superior Clubs in the Senior tourney.

Bell's Temperance F.C., now a defunct Club, were not only the first winners of the Junior Cup, but they won it the first two Seasons it was played for, and the L.F.A. Executive, as it was then called, decided that Bell's Temperance should be classified for the Senior Competition, When the Draw for the latter was made they were drawn to play Bolton Wanderers at Pike's Lane. There was great enthusiasm in the Bell's Camp—great preparations and great expectations—indeed on the eve of the match a number of Bell's Temperance supporters endeavoured to ascertain the result by means of table rapping, and the ceremony performed with due solemnity brought the joyful intelligence that they had to win by one goal to none. whereas in truth and in fact they actually lost the match the next day by ten goals to none.

Turton F.C., also now unfortunately defunct, was the earliest Lancashire Club to take up " Soccer " football, at any rate so far back as 1872 the Club had adopted the Harrow Rules, which are referred to elsewhere.  Turton F.C. won the Junior Cup on four occasions, Chorley F.C. having won it three times, and the following Clubs have won it twice each :—

Bell's Temperance.                    Heywood.
Blackpool.                            Skerton.
Earlestown.                           Morecambe.

and the following having won the Cup once each :—

Accrington Stanley.                   Horwich R.M.I.
Bacup.                                Lytham.
Blackburn Park Road.                  Nelson.
Bury.                                 New Brighton.
Clitheroe.                            Rochdale.
Colne                                 Rossendale United.
Croston.                              Runcorn.
Fleetwood.                            Skelmersdale United.
Hapton.                               Southport.
Kearsley.                             Oswaldtwistle.
Lancaster Town.

The Cup has therefore been won on forty occasions.

Lancaster Town have the remarkable experience of playing the following four Finals, and being beaten each time :—

1906-07 Beaten by Earlstown 3—1, after a drawn game of 1—1.

1908-09 Beaten by Chorley 4—2.

1919-20 Beaten by Southport 1—0.

1926-27 Beaten by Morecambe 1—0.

But at their fifth attempt on 28th January, 1928, they achieved their ambition, and thus became holders of the Cup in the Jubilee Year of the Association.

Skerton F.C. have a record of being in the Junior Cup Final Tie four consecutive Seasons, viz., 1895-96 and 1896-97, when they were beaten, and 1897-98 and 1898-99, when they won. The Skerton F.C., I think, hold another record in that they had in 1895-96 to meet four times to decide their Semi-Final Tie v. Haydock. The first match was a draw 1—1, the late John Lewis being the Referee. The second match had to be abandoned at half-time through a violent storm, the Referee being Mr. R. Watson. The third match with a draw at the end of 90 minutes, and Mr. R. Watson, who again refereed, ordered an extra 30 minutes play, and even then the match was a draw, a further 20 minutes were then played, and the score was still 2 goals each. The fourth meeting was on the Blackburn Rovers ground, when Skerton beat Haydock by 5 goals to 3, the tussle having lasted six hours and five minutes.

In the early years of the Competition the " glory " of winning the Cup was a greater concern than the financial return, and on a number of occasions Clubs have fought grimly, when the gross " gate " receipts have been beggarly.

On a number of occasions the receipts in Final Ties were round about £30, and if there was a £100 " gate " it was regarded as a great achievement. It is therefore of interest to note the following returns of Post-War Final Ties.

1919-20. Lancaster Town v. Southport, at Lancaster. £340/1/10.

1920-21. Accrington Stanley v. Chorley, at Ewood Park. £1,104/18/9.

1921-22. Chorley v. New Brighton, at Deepdale, £517/19/1; re-play at Bolton, £690/17/4.

1922-23. Croston v. Bacup Borough, at Deepdale. £235/14/2.

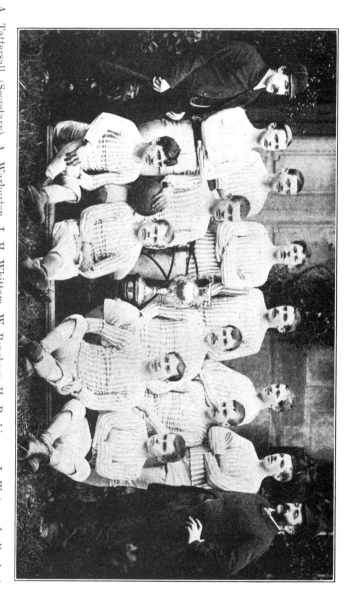

**BELL'S TEMPERANCE F.C.**

FIRST WINNERS OF LANCASHIRE JUNIOR CUP, 1885-86.

A. Tattersall (Secretary), A. Warburton, J. H. Whittam, W. Renshaw, H. Parkinson, J. Watson, L. Pemberton,
E. J. Holden (Chairman).
J. R. Swindlehurst (Captain), J. Heaton, L. Clarkson.
G. Law, G. Entwistle, E. Holgate, — Sproule.

1923-24. Chorley v. Barnoldswick Town, at Burnley. £275/14/8.

1924-25. Horwich R.M.I. v. Atherton, at Chorley. £172/6/9.

1925-26. Chorley v. Morecambe, at Preston, £492/1/3 replay at Bolton, £422/10/0; replay at Preston, £350/5/8.

These figures are very satisfactory, and must make previous Finalists sigh with envy, when they remember the small amounts they shared.

The Clubs belonging to the Lancashire Combination look upon the Junior Cup Competition as their own, and as a matter of fact the Competition is comprised almost entirely of such Clubs. There are, however, a number of outside Clubs, such as Adlington, Barrow Y.M.C.A., Breightmet United, Black Lane Rovers, Bootle, Bootle Celtic, Coppull Central, Horwich Central, Little Lever, Lytham, Portsmouth Rovers, Prescot, St. Helens Town, Skelmersdale United, Walsden United, and Ulverston Town, who regularly compete, and who occasionally, and very joyously, not only win an occasional round against Lancashire Combination Clubs, but who also win the Cup. That happened so recently as 1922-23, when Croston F.C., now defunct, but then playing in the West Lancashire League, went through the Competition. They beat Lancaster Town in the Semi-Final Tie, and then beat Bacup Borough in the Final.

The Junior Cup Ties have often given a new interest to a Club when its ordinary fixtures have begun to flag, it has given a zest to the players, and appealed to the competitive spirit of British sportsmen; such Ties have on a number of occasions brought players into the limelight, who would not have otherwise been seen. The writer can name more than one present-day professional player who holds an F.A. Cup Final Medal, and also a Lancashire Junior Cup Final Medal.

It will be a bad day for Senior football, if and when, Junior Cup Competitions cease to be played.

F

THE LANCASHIRE AMATEUR CUP.

# CHAPTER X.

*Lancashire Amateur Cup Competition. Matches in the early " eighties." Clubs first drawn in Amateur Cup. Nine Blackburn players in a Team v. Leicestershire. Amateur players who have become famous. Past Cup Winners. Formation of Northern Counties Amateur Championship.*

## LANCASHIRE AMATEUR CUP COMPETITION.

The Lancashire F.A. has more Senior Professional Clubs in its Membership than any other County Association, and that fact has sometimes been used by certain critics who have felt that the claims of Amateur Football were overlooked or neglected.

The work of the Association in 1878-84 was, however, entirely in the development of the game, and all players and Clubs were, of course, Amateurs.

Sham amateurism (or Shamateurs) brought about a crisis, and there was a big fight before The F.A. agreed to adopt the legalising of professionalism.

The Lancashire F.A. took a prominent part and gave a strong lead in this agitation, after which, it naturally strove to make the new feature of the game a success. The increased popularity of football after the adoption of professionalism was truly remarkable, but the Association never at any time forgot the claims of the Amateur Clubs.

In the early 'eighties, County matches were played with Cheshire, Nottingham, Northumberland, Lincolnshire, Staffordshire and Sussex, even though the playing of such games resulted in a financial loss to the Association. In 1892 it was felt that some steps should be taken to cater for the Amateur Clubs in other ways, and the Amateur Cup Competition was established.

The Draw for the First Round resulted as follows :—

| | |
|---|---|
| Birkdale South End | v. Liverpool Casuals. |
| Blackburn Etrurians | v. Preston Teachers. |
| Westhoughton Albion | v. Higher Walton. |
| Owens College | v. Darwen Olympic. |
| Eccles | v. Astley Bridge Wanderers. |

Byes :—Lytham, Aintree Church and Castleton.

The first winners of the Amateur Cup were Aintree Church, who beat Lytham by 3 goals to nil, the '' gate '' receipts being £11 16s. 6d. and the expenses £13.

The only present Member of The Lancashire F.A. who was connected with the promotion of the Competition is Mr. R. E. Lythgoe.

In the second Season of the Competition additional Clubs joined who left their mark on the Cup records, Liverpool Police Athletic, Liverpool Ramblers and Liverpool Leek, and in 1896 Old Xaverians became Competitors.

Of the Clubs named Mr. E. A. Morton, J.P., is still connected with the Competition, being a co-opted Member of the Council and a Member of the Amateur Cup Committee.  Mr. R. Nelson, who was Secretary of the Liverpool Police Athletic, is still a keen supporter of his Club, and is nearly always present at the Final Ties of the Competition.

The standard of play had become very high when the Great War intervened in 1914, and the Competition was at once withdrawn, and was not again played until 1919-20.

In some instances the players enlisted en bloc, and it can be imagined that there was considerable difficulty after the War in ascertaining what Clubs were in a position to resume.  For a few Seasons following the Great Conflict the play was not up to the usual standard of the Competition, but gradually it has risen to its previous excellence.

The number of players connected with the Competition who have turned professional is not large, but some of them have risen to the greatest heights possible.

**GEO. H. BARLOW.**
Wigan Amateurs A.F.C.

**R. SHIPPERBOTTOM.**
Old Boltonians A.F.C.

**H. P. HARDMAN.**
Everton F.C. and Manchester United F.C.
Now a member of Lancs. F.A. Council.

**N. JONES.**
Aldermere A.F.C.

# AINTREE CHURCH A.F.C.

## FIRST WINNERS OF LANCASHIRE AMATEUR CUP, 1893-94.

A. Lomax (Secretary), G. Stafford, R. Killop, R. Gratton, E. Hughes, J. Jones, J. Lynott (Trainer),
G. Martin, A. Jones, W. Gorman.
F. Meakin, C. Meakin, C. Jones.

E. Taylor, who has "kept" for England, and played with Oldham Athletic, Huddersfield Town and Everton, was previously connected with Liverpool Balmoral, and through his displays in Amateur Cup Ties was selected to keep goal for Lancashire in several Amateur County games.

Freeman, of Middlesbrough ; Hanson, of Manchester United ; Forrest, of Blackburn Rovers ; all played in matches connected with the Lancashire Amateur Cup Competition.

G. H. Barlow (Wigan Amateurs and Preston North End) ; H. P. Hardman (Everton) ; J. E. Blair (Collegiate Old Boys and Oldham Athletic) ; J. F. Mitchell (Manchester University, Blackpool, Preston North End and Manchester City) ; Roy Shipperbottom (Old Boltonians and Bolton Wanderers); Norman Jones (Aldermere and Manchester City); C. Moores (Crumpsall and Bury); C. G. Menham (Northern Nomands and Everton); T. Parker (Stalybridge Celtic and Everton); Max Woosnam (Manchester City), are men who have done great service to both Amateur and Professional Clubs, and yet retained their status as Amateurs.

The Amateur Cup Competition was (with the exception of two Seasons) always a great source of financial loss to the Association, from its inception until the Competition was held up in 1914, but since its resumption in 1919-20 the Final Ties have been most successful, several of them realising " gates " of over £100 each, and the thanks of the Association are due to the Everton and Liverpool Clubs, who have so often allowed their grounds to be used for the Final Ties.

Liverpool Police Athletic won the Cup five times, their last three victories being in 1922-23, 1923-24, 1924-25, Blackburn Etrurians, Preston Winckley, Ogdens Athletic, and Wigan Amateurs, each won the Cup twice in successive Seasons, and Blackburn Etrurians won the Cup four times in all.

## LIVERPOOL POLICE ATHLETIC F.C.
### WINNERS OF LANCASHIRE AMATEUR CUP, 1924-25.

Back Row (standing on form): F. Bradshaw, W. Jones, A. E. Millington, W. Cross (Captain), P. O'Hara (Committee).
Third Row: F. Addis (Committee), W. E. Sewell, W. S. Oliver, J. Pearson, P. Connell, G. Stevenson (Committee).
Second Row: J. Pimblett, L. D. L. Everett, Esq. (Chief Constable), W. Smith, J. Horne (Committee), W. H. Jennings.
Front Row: D. Woosey, W. Brackley.

[PHOTO BY " CARBONORA " CO., LIVERPOOL.]

The full list of winners is as follows :—

1893-94—Aintree Church.
94-95—Liverpool Police Athletic.
95-96—Blackburn Etrurians.
96-97—Liverpool Casuals.
97-98—Liverpool Police Athletic.
98-99—Blackburn Etrurians.
99-1900—Blackburn Etrurians.
1900-01—Bury Atheneaum.
01-02—Liverpool Casuals.
02-03—Blackburn Cross Hill.
03-04—Lytham Institute.
04-05—Blackburn Etrurians.
05-06—Fleetwood Amateurs.
06-07—Chorlton-cum-Hardy.
07-08—Preston Winckley.
08-09—Preston Winckley.
09-10—Wigan Amateurs.
10-11—Wigan Amateurs.
11-12—Manchester South End.
12-13—Ogden's Athletic.
13-14—Ogden's Athletic.
14-15 ⎫
15-16 ⎪ Not played for in con-
16-17 ⎬ sequence of the great
17-18 ⎪ European War.
18-19 ⎭
19-20—Manchester University.
20-21—Liverpool University.
21-22—Marine.
22-23—Liverpool Police Athletic.
23-24—Liverpool Police Athetic.
24-25—Liverpool Police Athletic.
25-26—Marine.
26-27—Earle.
27-28—Cadby Hall.

## AMATEUR  COUNTY  MATCHES.

Since 1900 many Counties have been met, including, Cheshire, Birmingham A.F.A., Cumberland, Leicestershire, West Riding and London, but it is to be regretted that more interest has not been taken by the public.

In 1910-11 Birmingham A.F.A. were entertained at Rochdale, the match being freely advertised in the Press and on the hoardings, and the necessary arrangements for Checkers, attendance of Police, etc., being duly made. The gross " gate " was £1 12s. 9d.

In 1905 there were no less than seven players connected with Blackburn Etrurians and Blackburn Cross Hill selected to play in an Amateur County Match v. Leicestershire, and through injuries, etc., nine Blackburn players actually played, the Team being :—F. Ward (Cross Hill) ; W. Hoghton (Etrurians), A. L. Bryham (Hesketh Park) ; H. Slater (Cross Hill), F. Walmsley, Captain, (Etrurians), H. Woolfall (Cross Hill); W. Crabtree (Etrurians), R. G. Brandwood (Cross Hill), W. Nuttall (Etrurians), H. C. A. Pratt (Old Xaverians), A. Dawson (Cross Hill).

The County Matches v. West Riding F.A. played at Accrington in 1920-21, and at Lancaster in 1922-23 and in 1924-25, were well supported, and were very fine exhibitions.

A stimulus to Amateur Football was given in 1925, when the Northern Counties Amateur Championship was formed, the Competition comprising the following Associations :—Cumberland, Cheshire, East Riding, Lancashire, Liverpool, Manchester, Sheffield and Hallamshire and West Riding.

The obstacles in the way were at first very considerable, but thanks to Mr. C. E. Sutcliffe, who was then Deputy-President, in the absence of the late Mr. J. Lewis, a constitution was agreed upon and the Competition duly formed.

The Competition is on the knock-out principle, and the first winners were Cheshire County F.A.

**BLACKBURN ETRURIANS A.F.C.**

WINNERS OF LANCASHIRE AMATEUR CUP, 1899-1900.

J. Hunter (Trainer), W. Lawrence, F. Carmichael, R. Dickinson, W. Halliday, W. Neville, A. D. Gorse. Seated: B. Sutcliffe, O. Gillett, W. Briggs, R. Cooper, F. Davies, E. Makinson, A. Briggs.

NORTHERN COUNTIES AMATEUR CHAMPIONSHIP TROPHY.

PRESENTED BY LANCASHIRE FOOTBALL ASSOCIATION. 1925-26.

The Lancashire F.A. provided the trophy for the Competition, and, as will be seen from the photograph shown on page 88, it is unique in character, being a silver ball mounted on a miniature field, with goal posts also in silver.

The President of Lancashire F.A., despite his many connections with professional organisations, takes a lively interest in all the arrangements and matches of the Amateur Cup, and of Amateur County matches, and he has the loyal co-operation and support of the following Council Members of the Amateur Cup Committee :—Messrs. T. Laithwaite, T. P. Campbell, J. Taylor, F. Morris, J. Kenny, W. J. Sawyer, J. W. Haworth and E. A. Morton, J.P., together with the co-opted Members : Messrs. S. E. Woollam and J. H. Scroggie.

THE LANCASHIRE JUNIOR CHALLENGE SHIELD.

# CHAPTER XI.

## THE LANCASHIRE JUNIOR SHIELD COMPETITION.

*Its inception. The first Winners. Record " gate " in 1922-23. How the Finalists have benefited, and how competing Teams are assisted.*

The Junior Shield Competition was instituted in 1906. It was proposed by the late Mr. John James Haworth, a Turton worthy, who served on The Lancashire F.A. Council from 1901 until he died in 1909.

The object of the Shield Competition was to partly relieve the Junior Cup Competition from too big an entry, no less than 70 Clubs having entered for the Junior Cup in 1906, and therefore a further Competition was necessary in which the Clubs would more or less have a reasonable chance of success. The Shield was competed for by 39 Clubs in 1906-07, when the Finalists were Hindley Green and Hindley Central, the gross receipts being £17 10s. 10d.

In 1922-23, when Atherton Collieries and Barnoldswick Town played in the Final Tie at Burnden Park, the gross receipts were £205 9s. 6d., which is a record for the Competition.

It is not generally known that The Lancashire F.A. does not benefit one penny from the Shield Competition. The Clubs in the Final Tie receive the entire " gate " receipts after the Tax, ground and advertising expenses have been paid. The 38 Clubs who have played in the Shield Final Ties have shared a total of £772 1s. 1d.

When a Final Tie has resulted in a financial loss, Grants of £10 to each Club have been made from the Association Funds.

Seven Shield Final Ties have been played at Burnden Park ground, which is generally a very convenient centre, no doubt the fact that there are more entries from Bolton and District than from any other area has conduced to the success of the Bolton Clubs, and of the Competition.

The players who take part in the Final Tie all receive gold medals, which are paid for out of the Association's Funds.  Clubs who fail to reach the Final Tie have the right to ask the Association to make good any loss sustained in playing in the Competition, and each Season between £20 to £30 is paid to the Clubs who so apply

If you really want to see an exciting football match, a game with 22 triers, with each team supported by its " fans," to see a real demonstration of Club partisanship and of abounding enthusiasm, then you should visit a Lancashire Junior Shield Final Tie ;   at any rate the representatives (or scouts) of Clubs from all parts of England have often been seen at these gatherings, and a number of players have thereby won their entry to Senior Football.

The average entry for the Competition is 100, but there is no reason why that number should not be exceeded.  The Clubs are drawn in geographical groups in the early rounds, and therefore it is only in the later stages of the Competition that the Clubs have to travel beyond their local areas.

The Shield was not played for during Seasons 1915-16, 1916-17 and 1917-18, because of the Great War.

**HINDLEY CENTRAL F.C.**

FIRST WINNERS, JUNIOR SHIELD, 1906-7.

Back Row: P. Winstanley, W. Knowles, J. Sargeant, J. Gaskell, H. Heyes, T. Pyke.
Front Row: J. Talbot, T. Smith, B. Grundy, H. Foster, W. Settle.

**BLACK LANE ROVERS F.C.**

JUNIOR SHIELD WINNERS, 1923-24.

S. Crossley (Trainer), A. Gregory, J. Mort, A. Leach, A. Hardman.
W. Kennedy (Captain), P. Allen, H. Mort, S. Howarth.
J. Brown, A. Greenhalgh, J. Hampson, L. Peatfield, R. Seddon.

# CHAPTER XII.

## CHRONOLOGICAL EVENTS.

Extracts from the Minutes of the Association, which speak for themselves, 1878-1889.

April 26th, 1879.

Unanimously resolved, " That a Challenge Cup be bought."

June 14th, 1879.

Resolved, " That the Manchester and County Bank, and its Branches, be the Bankers for the Association."

August 16th, 1879.

Resolved to apply to The F.A. for membership.

"Read letter from T. Eastwood, Secretary to Blackburn Rovers, informing the Committee that Richard Birtwistle would represent his Club in future in place of John Lewis."

First Draw for the Lancashire Cup made at the " Coffee Tavern," Darwen Street, Blackburn.

September 6th, 1879.

First Annual Meeting. The Report contained the following :—" From the Balance Sheet it appeared that £77 12s. 11d. had been received by the Association from all sources, whilst the expenditure amounted to £84 5s. 7d., which, with amounts still owing, amounting to say £3 7s. 7d., showed a clear loss of £10 on the year's workings. The Balance Sheet, which was signed by J. Mangnall (Eagley) and F. Y. Singleton (Darwen Rangers) as the Auditors, was then put to the Meeting and passed."

The Second Annual Meeting reported a balance of £14 18s. 5d.

OCTOBER 22ND, 1879.

W. Forrest and T. Dixon promised £5 each, R. Green promised £1 and T. Hindle promised £10 towards the cost of the Lancashire Cup.

NOVEMBER 22ND, 1879.

T. Duxbury moved, and R. Birtwistle seconded, " That a representative of the Association be chosen to represent Lancashire on the Committee of The F.A.," but after a short discussion an amendment was proposed, " That this be not entertained until such times as the Association can afford to pay expenses of a representative." The amendment was carried.

However, on April 21st, 1880, it was " Resolved that the Secretary represent the Association on The F. A. in London."

FEBRUARY 14TH, 1880.

Design of Lancashire Cup accepted and approved. The design of Monk Bros., Bolton, was accepted, the price being £118, and the weight of the Cup 170-180ozs., later the cost was increased to £160.

Mr. T. Hindle, in tendering his second annual report on September 4th, 1880, also tendered his resignation, whereupon the Committee accepted the report with the exception of the reference to the Secretary's resignation, and Mr. Hindle was asked to retire. Upon being recalled to the room he was informed, " That he (Mr. Hindle) had been re-appointed Hon. Secretary to the Association, and that at the end of the Season (1880-81) he be allowed £30 for his private expenses, should there be funds sufficient to pay him with." The Secretary accepted the office for another Season at their request, but the £30 was not paid, as the Association sustained a loss that Season.

NOVEMBER 15TH, 1880.

Protest made by Everton F.C. against the win claimed by Great Lever, on the ground that the Referee was a

Member of the Great Lever Club, and was therefore biased in their favour.

The protest was sustained and the match " ordered to be played over."

On December 11th, 1880, Mr. T. Hindle again tendered his resignation because of adverse criticism by Blackburn Rovers and Darwen, and also by certain Members of the Association Committee, but he was prevailed upon to withdraw his resignation.

JANUARY 18TH, 1881.

Reported, " That the funds of the Association are very low," and considered " what steps to take to get an overdraft at the Bank."

" Mr. Bury kindly offered to lend the Association £50," and " his kind offer was accepted with thanks."

MAY 3RD, 1881.

" Letter from Blackburn Rovers resigning as Members of the Association, and after some discussion it was resolved that the Secretary send a formal acceptance of same."

MAY 28TH, 1881.

Resolved, "That Clubs, Members of the Association, be requested not to arrange any fixtures with Blackburn Rovers for this Season."

MAY 28TH, 1881.

Mr. T. Hindle was again elected Secretary.

JUNE 18TH, 1881.

" Letter from Blackburn Rovers applying to rejoin the Association," the Club having sent the following letter, " That a proposition be made to the Lancashire F.A. to let bygones be bygones, to rejoin the Association, and to do all in our power to assist in carrying out its Rules in the interests of the County."

After a short discussion it was unanimously decided "that the Rovers be re-admitted, and that all bygones be bygones."

In January and February, 1880, Blackburn Rovers had a prolonged dispute with Turton over a Lancashire Cup Tie, there was protest and counter protest, at one meeting the "matter was discussed in all its phases," the discussion lasting one hour and a half."

The Rovers were evidently dissatisfied, for on February 6th, 1880, it was reported, " Letter was read from Blackburn Rovers stating that unless the decision of the Committee in regard to the Turton protest is rescinded, they (the Rovers) would not permit the use of their ground for the match v. London."

It was resolved that the Association Secretary should meet the Rovers and explain the position. As evidence of the length of the meeting we read, " The Secretary be allowed a cab home in consequence of there being no trains."

JUNE 30TH, 1881.

Arrangements sanctioned for an " over-draft of £150."

OCTOBER 6TH, 1881.

Darwen F.C. withdrew from The L.F.A. Cup Competition because of the dispute with Blackburn Rovers.

MARCH 14TH, 1882.

It was reported that Mr. Hindle had definitely declined to continue as Secretary. It was thereupon decided to advertise in the " Athletic News " and in the Bolton and Darwen papers for a Secretary, the salary to be £50.

MAY 15TH, 1882.

Eighteen applications for the post of Secretary were considered, and the Committee having heard the letters of application proceeded to vote; ten were eliminated on the first vote, and four more were struck out on a second vote, leaving J. J. Bentley, Bolton ; J. Norburn, Bolton ; T. Heald, Accrington ; and R. P. Gregson, Blackburn, to be further voted upon, and the latter was recommended for appointment.

At the Annual Meeting on 27th May, 1882, the Sub-Committee's Report was disagreed with, and the following were nominated for the Secretaryship :—Messrs. J. J. Bentley, W. Bramham, T. Heald and R. P. Gregson, and after Mr. Bramham and Mr. Heald had been eliminated the final vote was taken, when 32 voted for Mr. Gregson and 13 for Mr. Bentley, and therefore Mr. Gregson secured the appointment.

OCTOBER 23RD, 1882.

Meeting at " White Bull," Blackburn. " There being no quorum, no business was done."

DECEMBER 13TH, 1882.

Mr. T. Hindle was presented with an illuminated address signed by the President, Lord Hartington, and the Vice-Presidents of the Association, also presented with a gold watch, guard and locket, and a cheque for £36.

APRIL 6TH, 1883.

" That the Committee of The Lancashire F.A. tender their hearty congratulations to the Blackburn Olympic Football Club on their success in winning The Football Association Challenge Cup. By the victory they have done honour to themselves as well as to the County."

APRIL 1ST, 1884.

" The Secretary was instructed to tender the congratulations of the Committee to the Blackburn Rovers on the occasion of their winning The F.A. Challenge Cup."

ANNUAL MEETING, 1885.

Blackburn Rovers F.C. congratulated on again winning The F.A. Cup.

**PRESTON NORTH END F.C.**

F.A. CUP WINNERS, 1888-9.

G. Drummond, R. H. Howarth, Mr. R. W. Hanbury, M.P., Mr. W. E. Tomlinson, M.P., D. Russell, R. Holmes, W. Sudell
(Chairman), J. Graham, R. H. Mills-Roberts.
J. Gordon, J. Ross, J. Goodall, F. Dewhurst, S. Thomson.

Minute from the Annual Meeting held at Blackburn in April, 1886 :—" An elderly gentleman from Chipping attended to represent the club of that place. Last year, he said, it appeared that the Association objected to clubs going to their ground to play, through being so far from the railway. He was deputed to say that clubs coming to play would be met by a pair of horses and a wagonette at Longridge, and conveyed to and from Chipping at railway rates. The Chairman, Mr. Forrest, said the objection would be withdrawn after the generous offer which had been made."

ANNUAL MEETING, 1886.

Blackburn Rovers F.C. congratulated on again winning The F.A. Cup, which feat they had accomplished three seasons in succession.

1886 ONWARD.

Many County matches were played—professional players taking part against such teams as :—Dumbarton-shire, Staffordshire ,Nottinghamshire, North Wales, Ulster, Northumberland, Lincolnshire and Birmingham.

1886 TO 1900.

Most of the work—causing innumerable long meetings —was that of dealing with protests and counter protests.

Preston North End refused to play in a Lancashire Cup Tie at Blackburn in 1888, because " of the attitude of the Blackburn spectators on a previous occasion."

On April 23rd, 1888, Preston North End were sus-pended to December 31st, 1888, and the facts reported to The F.A.

On May 3rd, 1888, it was reported that The F.A. had refused to endorse North End's suspension, which re-sulted in not only The Lancashire F.A. altering their Rules to state, " No Club shall be allowed to ' scratch ' in the Semi-Final or Final Ties," but The F.A. also made the same revision of their Rules.

The Revision of Rules was evidently a matter of great care in the 'eighties, for we find that a Rules Revision Committee had the following meetings :—Met at Blackpool on 11th August, 1888, sat four hours, and adjourned. Met at Wigan on 14th August, 1888, and sat three hours, and adjourned. Met at Blackburn on 15th August, 1888, and sat for two hours.

Annual Meeting, 1889.

Preston North End F.C. congratulated on winning The F.A. Cup.

Annual Meeting, 1890.

Blackburn Rovers F.C. congratulated on winning The F.A. Cup for the fourth time.

Annual Meeting, 1891.

Blackburn Rovers F.C. congratulated on winning The F.A. Cup for the fifth time.

# CHAPTER XIII.

## FURTHER EXTRACTS FROM MINUTES OF THE ASSOCIATION, 1889—1920.

JANUARY 31ST, 1889.

South Shore F.C. were responsible for a Rule being inserted in The F.A. Cup Rules. They had joined The F.A. Cup Competition and were drawn to meet Chatham, who entertained them on a public field where no " gate " money could be charged.

The South Shore F.C. complained to The Lancashire F.A., and the latter sent a resolution to The F.A. stating, " A Club not having an enclosed ground where " gate " money may be taken should play on its opponents' ground."

AUGUST 21ST, 1891.

Bury F.C. promoted from the Junior Cup Competition to the Senior Cup Competition, and Liverpool was ad-mitted to it the following year.

OCTOBER 1ST, 1891.

" The President (Mr. W. Forrest) was presented with a pair of white gloves as there had not been any protests in the 1st Round of the Lancashire Cup Competition.

MARCH, 1893.

BURY v. BOLTON WANDERERS. LANCASHIRE CUP TIE.

Bury F.C. reported for the crowd encroaching, and in defence stated this was their largest " gate," 14,700 paid for admission. The match was ordered to be re-played at Bolton.

3RD JULY, 1893.

Amateur Cup Competition Rules approved.

**BLACKBURN ROVERS F.C.**
WINNERS OF THE F.A. CUP, 1883-4.

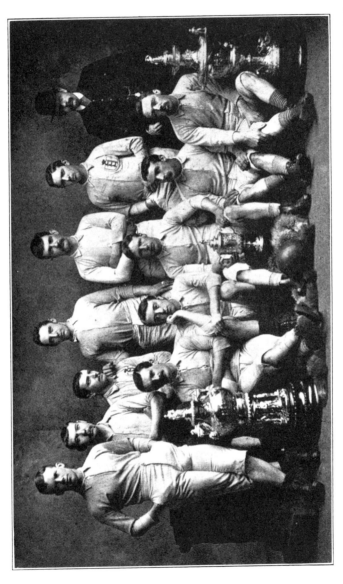

Back Row: J. Lofthouse, H. McIntyre, J. Beverley, H. Arthur, F. Suter, J. B. Forrest, R. Birtwistle (Umpire).
Front Row: J. Douglas, J. Sowerbutts, J. Brown, G. Avery, J. Hargreaves.
Trophies: East Lancashire Charity Cup, Football Association Cup, L.F.A. Cup.

JANUARY, 1895.

A circular issued to all clubs re " growing number of players being reported for misconduct," and asking for " co-operation in stopping this ungentlemanly and unsportsmanlike conduct."

Notices to be posted in dressing rooms, etc.

In 1895 Manchester City played a second team in a Lancashire Cup Tie, with the result that at the subsequent Annual Meeting the following was added to the Lancashire Cup Rules : " A Club must play it's full strength in all Cup Ties."

MAY 11TH, 1896.

A sum of £25 was voted for the purpose of a Wedding Present for Mr. T. Hindle.

SEPTEMBER 23RD, 1896.

Consent given for Manchester and District F.A. to become affiliated to The F.A.

1899.

Medal Competitions established, and the L.F.A. held several meetings dealing with their sanction and control.

L.F.A. celebrated its 21st Anniversary at the Saddle Hotel, Bolton, on September 28th, 1899, when the Executive had a Dinner.

1900.

Bury F.C. congratulated on winning The F.A. Cup.

MARCH 1ST, 1901.

Accrington Stanley suspended until they " fixed the blame " in connection with the " gate " receipts of a Junior Cup Second Round Tie having been tampered with.

It was proved " that at least £5 19s. 0d. had been improperly retained."

Eventually four persons were named, and they were suspended, one for five years, and three for two years each, and the suspension on the Club was removed.

On April 30th, 1901, the L.F.A. attempted to amalga-
mate the Lancashire League and Lancashire Combination,
and tabled a scheme with the clubs in two divisions, North
and South.

The Lancashire Combination, however, rejected the
scheme.

1902-3.

Bury F.C. congratulated on again winning The F.A.
Cup.

1903-04.

Manchester City F.C. congratulated on winning The
F.A. Cup.

MAY 18TH, 1904.

A. H. Downs, Secretary of Lancashire Combination,
elected an Hon. Auditor of the Association.

MAY 24TH, 1905.

Long Service Medals presented to :—

D. B. Woolfall, 24 years' service.

T. Hindle, 27 years' service.

T. Duxbury, 27 years' service.

J. S. Roscow, 21 years' service.

J. J. Cooper, 21 years' service.

R. P. Gregson, 23 years' service.
    (Secretary).

AUGUST 22ND, 1905.

Model Rules drawn up for the government and control
of Leagues.

MAY 23RD, 1906.

Everton F.C. congratulated on winning The F.A. Cup.
Lancashire Junior Shield Competition established.

MAY 9TH, 1907.

A Referee fined 5s. and suspended two months for
allowing an Everton player to remain on the field after he
had been ordered off.

SEPTEMBER 18TH, 1907.

Presentation to R. P. Gregson in recognition of twenty-five years' service.

After a Meeting of the Council held at the Saddle Hotel, Bolton, on September 18th, 1907, a presentation was made to Mr. Gregson. 120 Clubs and Leagues were represented.

FEBRUARY, 1908.

A Commission held with reference to the serious financial position of Barrow F.C.

FEBRUARY, 1908.

Mr. J. Kenny reported Stalybridge Rovers for foul language by Club Officials after a match played v. Nelson on 15th February, 1908, and he also reported that for a time they refused to pay him his fee.

Four of the Officials were each suspended for 7 weeks, and the incident caused a recommendation to be made that in future Clubs must take the Officials' fees to them in the dressing room.

JUNE 1ST, 1908.

Presentation to Mr. F. Hargreaves (then Assistant to R. P. Gregson) on the occasion of his marriage.

SEPTEMBER, 1908.

Clubs and Leagues again circularised, calling attention to the large number of players reported, and intimating that "the Association is determined to stamp out improper conduct and dirty play."

MAY 6TH, 1909.

Great increase in the work of the Association reported at the Annual Meeting.

MAY 6TH, 1909.

J. Lewis completed 21 years' service and presented with his Long Service Medal.

Manchester United congratulated on having won The F.A. Cup.

MAY 4TH, 1910.

F. Hargreaves appointed Registrar of Referees in place of Mr. J. T. Howcroft who had resigned.

OCTOBER 25TH, 1910.

As Mr. R. P. Gregson had given up his studio in Blackburn, it was necessary for the Association to secure offices. Rooms at 42, Ainsworth Street, Blackburn, were secured.

APRIL 3RD, 1911.

R. P. Gregson resigned.

APRIL 11TH, 1911.

Messrs. D. B. Woolfall, J. J. Cooper, J. S. Roscow, J. J. Bentley, J. Lewis, W. E. Ord, T. Hindle, J. McKenna, and C. E. Sutcliffe, appointed to deal with the appointment of a new Secretary.

APRIL 26TH, 1911.

The Sub-Committee recommended F. Hargreaves be appointed Secretary, and the recommendation was unanimously endorsed by the Council.

SEPTEMBER, 1912.

Death of Tom Houghton, of Preston.

OCTOBER 9TH, 1912.

Burnley F.C. written to for " alleged not trying " in Lancashire Cup Competition.

Bolton Wanderers reported for unsatisfactory advertising.

Bury, Liverpool, Manchester City, Manchester United, and Preston North End, for playing weak teams.

City were fined twenty guineas, Bolton fined fifteen guineas, and the explanations from the other Clubs accepted. .

MAY 21ST, 1913.

Messrs. W. A. Duckworth, R. E. Lythgoe, and R. Watson presented with Long Service Medals.

JUNE 25TH, 1913.

Reported that Darwen F.C. had not joined the Junior Cup Competition, it was decided to inform the Club that unless they competed, objection would be taken to their playing in The F.A. Cup Competition.

JANUARY, 1914.

Death of H. S. Hamer, of Bury, Hon. Auditor of the Association since 1904.

JANUARY, 1914.

T. Charnley, Secretary of The Football League, elected as Hon. Auditor of The Association.

APRIL 9TH, 1914.

Instructions given for a junior player at Darwen to be prosecuted by a referee who had been assaulted in a Darwen Medal Competition match. The defendant was fined 20/- and costs.

MAY 16TH, 1914.

Unusual interest was taken in the Annual Meeting held at Blackpool, there being opposition to the divisional members in six out of the eight divisions, and the voting was very even. Mr. T. Laithwaite not only headed the poll for Division 7, but the whole of the 133 Clubs and Leagues at the Meeting voted for him.

Burnley F.C. congratulated on winning The F.A. Cup.

AUGUST 4TH, 1914.

Commencement of the Great War.

SEPTEMBER 2ND, 1914.

Letter from Manchester United suggesting that football grounds be offered for Military drilling, etc.

SEPTEMBER 8TH, 1914.

The Lancashire F.A. circularised all Clubs and Leagues, asking for co-operation in recruiting and for football grounds to be used for Military purposes.

H

September and October, 1914.

44 Clubs and 7 Leagues intimated they had ceased playing consequent upon the enlistment of players.

November and December, 1914.

Three more Leagues and 30 Clubs announced that they had suspended operations.

March 10th, 1915.

A Special General Meeting of the Association was held at Bolton, when the Rules of the Association were variously altered, the most important alteration being that the divisional members should retire in alternate years, instead of the previous system of all the divisional members retiring together.

May 15th, 1915.

Annual Meeting held at Bolton. Mr. T. Y. Ritson elected Hon. Treasurer vice Mr. T. Hindle, who was defeated by 39 votes to 17.

Return presented by the Secretary, F. Hargreaves, showing that 4,758 players and officials had joined His Majesty's Forces.

July 21st, 1915.

Decided to discontinue the Association's Competitions, in consequence of the Great War, also an Emergency Committee consisting of Messrs. D. B. Woolfall, J. Lewis, J. McKenna, and the Secretary, appointed to act as required, instead of the usual Meetings of the Council.

1916-17 and 1917-18.

No Annual Meetings of the Association held.

February 20th, 1918.

A Meeting of the Council held at Bolton, this being the first since 21st July, 1915.

**EVERTON F.C.**

WINNERS OF THE F.A. CUP, 1905-06.

Standing: A. R. Wade (Director), H. Makepeace, W. C. Cuff (Secretary), A. Young, J. Davies (Director),
E. A. Bainbridge (Director), J. D. Taylor, G. Mahon (Director), W. Scott, B. Kelly (Director),
W. Balmer, H. Wright (Director), J. Elliott (Trainer).

Seated: W. R. Clayton (Director), Dr. J. C. Baxter (Director), J. Sharp, H. Bolton, W. Abbott, J. Settle,
J. Crelley, H. P. Hardman, Dr. W. Whitford (Director), D. Kirkwood (Director).

ATHERTON COLLIERIES F.C.
JUNIOR SHIELD WINNERS, 1922-23.

A. Coulton (Trainer), A. McDonough, H. Brown, J. Ford, S. Loveless (Assist. Trainer),
T. Virgo, N. Pedley, N. Monoghan.
W. May, T. Hook, A. Harris, H. Butler, W. Roberts.

## ANNUAL MEETING, JUNE 5TH, 1918.

Deaths reported of James Cooper, William Heath and Peter Ward, Members of the Council, also of R. P. Gregson, the previous Secretary.

A Re-organisation Committee appointed to assist in the re-establishment of football, and in fostering and assisting minor and junior football.

## NOVEMBER 18TH, 1918.

The Secretary reported that since the last meeting there had died D. B. Woolfall, President of the Association, J. S. Roscow, J. J. Bentley, Vice-Presidents, and W. A. Duckworth, Representative of Division 4.

J. Lewis was elected President and C. E. Sutcliffe, J. McKenna, and R. Watson, were elected Vice-Presidents.

The Junior Cup and Junior Shield Competitions were revived.

## APRIL, 1919.

The death reported of J. A. MacGregor, Representative of Division 8.

Mr. Sutcliffe's emergency Lancashire Cup scheme adopted, and the Competition a huge success.

## JUNE 16TH, 1919.

Annual Meeting held at Bolton, when it was reported that the financial stability of the Association had been re-established.

Mr. J. J. Cooper resigned his position as a Vice-President, and Mr. Richard Birtwistle was elected in his place.

Amnesty on suspended players. In celebration of the end of the Great War, it was decided to remove all suspensions imposed on players by this Association.

The Association Benevolent Fund re-established. £100 being transferred from the General funds of the Association, a further £100 being voted in March, 1920.

SEPTEMBER—DECEMBER, 1919.

Great influx of new Clubs and Leagues. The Secretary given permission to have the services of a junior clerk.

JUNE 16TH, 1919 .

£128 13s. 0d. repaid to the Secretary, F. Hargreaves, this being the amount of his loss by reduction of salary during the War, and which he had voluntarily surrendered.

AUGUST, 1919.

Scheme formulated for the fostering of juvenile football, Cups being offered to all Education Authorities in Lancashire.

OCTOBER, 1919.

Cups provided for Barrow Juvenile Committee and Wigan Juvenile Committee, and a Cup and two sets of medals for the Lancashire Elementary Schools Competition.

DECEMBER, 1920.

Additional office staff sanctioned in view of the great increase in the work of the Association.

Many Clubs dealt with and fined for making irregular payments to Amateur players, and 55 players declared professionals.

# CHAPTER XIV.

## FURTHER EXTRACTS FROM THE MINUTES OF THE ASSOCIATION, 1920—1928.

MARCH 3RD, 1920.

A defendant fined 40/- and costs for an assault on a Burnley Referee, the proceedings being instituted by the Association.

JUNE 5TH, 1920.

Annual Meeting held at Blackpool, when it was reported that the Lancashire Cup Competition had again been a great success.

SEPTEMBER, 1921.

All Clubs directly and indirectly connected with the Association requested to display notices on their grounds and in their dressing rooms, appealing to the players to play the game in a fair and proper manner.

Furness District F.A. authorised to deal with Referees Reports, and of all cases arising within their area.

DECEMBER, 1921.

A player was suspended for life for " biting " an opponent. At first the Commission thought the offence was " hitting an opponent," and it was some time before they could realise the peculiarity of this unusually brutal assault.

SHIELD PROTEST—JANUARY, 1922.

The protesting Club claimed that a player named Walter H——— had played against them, and that he was ineligible. After a prolonged investigation it was ascertained that the player who attended the Commission as Walter H———, was not that person, but had assumed that name to confuse the protestors. Eventually it was found that an ineligible player had played, and his identity was only established after reference to his war time ration

card, his National Registration card, and   his   National
Health Insurance card.

The offending Club was suspended.

APRIL, 1922.

A prominent Senior Club was dealt with for allowing
Medal Competition matches to be decided on corner kicks,
when matches had resulted in draws.

A more junior club had also allowed its Medal Competition Final Tie to be decided by " tossing " because
the match resulted in a draw.   The team who won the
" toss " were very reluctant to return the medals   when
ordered, and it took several months to secure their return.

JUNE, 1922.

Presentation of Long Service Medal to T. Y. Ritson.

AUGUST, 1922.

Cup provided for Lancashire Schoolboys.

JANUARY, 1923.

Cup provided for Preston Schoolboys.

ANNUAL MEETING, 1923.

Bolton Wanderers F.C. congratulated on winning The
F.A. Cup.

1923-24.

The Lancashire Cup Competition again played as a
Knock Out Competition in its entirety, instead of ascertaining the Semi-Finals on results of their Football League
games.

AUGUST 16TH, 1923.

Cup provided for Junior Section of Oldham and
District S.S. League.

MAY 24TH, 1924.

Resolved that " Paid officials of Clubs nominated for
the first time after May 24th, 1924, shall not be eligible
for election to the Council," but this resolution was
rescinded in 1926.

AUGUST 14TH, 1924.

Jubilee arrangements proposed. A Jubilee History
to be compiled. A Jubilee Match to be played, and a
Jubilee Banquet to be held.

**R. P. GREGSON.**
Second Secretary of Lancashire F.A.
1882-1911.

**T. HOUGHTON.**
Member of L.F.A. Council.
1905-1912.

**T. LAITHWAITE.**
Fifth and Present Hon. Treasurer of
Lancashire F.A.
Elected to Council 1904.

**R. E. LYTHGOE.**
Vice-President of The F.A. and Elected
Vice-President of Lancashire F.A. 1918.
Elected to Council 1892.

**T. Y. RITSON.**
Elected Vice-President of Lancashire
F.A. 1926. Hon. Treasurer 1919-1926.
Elected to Council 1901

**E. LITTLE.**
Elected Vice-President of Lancashire
F.A. 1927. Hon. Treasurer 1926-27.
Elected to Council 1904.

**R. WATSON.**
Member of The F.A. and Elected Vice-
President of Lancashire F.A. 1918.
Elected to Council 1892.

Messrs. C. E. Sutcliffe, J. Lewis, R. Birtwistle, R. Watson, and E. Webster, were appointed to consider the preliminary arrangements.

SEPTEMBER 25TH, 1924.

Resolved to purchase 42, St. George's Place, Blackburn, at a cost of £1,400, for the Offices of the Association. the Association.

JANUARY 29TH, 1925.

The new Offices opened by Mr. J. Lewis then President of the Association.

Income Tax demand for £484 0s. 9d.

Mr. C. E. Sutcliffe was appointed to act as Deputy President during the absence of Mr. J. Lewis, when away on the Australian tour.

MARCH 26TH, 1925.

Mr. J. Lewis entertained to Dinner in celebration of his 70th birthday, and also in honour of his appointment as Member in charge of the English Team to visit Australia.

Mr. Lewis was also presented with a Silver Gilt Casket and an Illuminated Scroll, and he was also elected a Life Member of the Association.

JUNE, 1925.

Presentation of Long Service Medals to T. Laithwaite and E. Little.

AUGUST 13TH, 1925.

Resolved to join the Northern Counties Amateur Championship, and also to provide a Trophy for the Competition.

JANUARY 13TH, 1926.

Death of Mr. J. Lewis, President.

JANUARY 21ST, 1926.

Mr. C. E. Sutcliffe elected President.

APRIL, 1926.

Bolton Wanderers congratulated on again winning The F.A. Cup.

January 20th, 1927.

Resolved to place on record that N. Tattersall, of Bury Amateurs, who played centre-forward for Lancashire v. Birmingham A.F.A., scored three goals in the first two minutes and fifteen seconds of the match played at Preston on 8th January, 1927, and that he scored a total of seven goals.

February 24th, 1927.

Cup provided for Atherton Schoolboys and also one for Bolton Boys' Federation.

June, 1927.

Death of T. Hindle, a founder of the Association, the first Secretary and Hon. Treasurer for 31 years.

June 23rd, 1927.

Mr. R. Birtwistle resigned his position as a Vice-President, he was elected a Life Member of the Association, and on 17th August, 1927, he was presented with a Silver Casket.

November 9th, 1927.

An appeal issued on behalf of the victims of the Fleetwood Flood Disaster, and £1,133 9s. 5d. was quickly raised.

May, 1928.

Everton F.C. congratulated on becoming Champions of The Football League, 1st Division.

Manchester City F.C. congratulated on becoming Champions of The Football League, 2nd Division.

Blackburn Rovers F.C. congratulated on winning The F.A. Cup for the sixth time.

May 12th, 1928.

Mr. Justice Hawke attended Lancashire Cup Final Tie, Bury v. Manchester City, played at Old Trafford, and presented the Cup to Manchester City F.C.

June 4th, 1928.

Minimum of 10/- for professionals abolished by The F.A., after prolonged agitation by Lancashire F.A.

LANCASHIRE F.A. COUNCIL AT LYTHAM, AUGUST, 1925.

Back Row: J. Taylor, T. P. Campbell, E. Clayton, J.P., E. Little, R. A. Beeley, J. W. Haworth.   [PHOTO BY R. JONES.]
Third Row: H. Sutcliffe (not a member of the Council), T. A. Barcroft, H. Windle, H. Duckworth, J. E. Mangnall.
Second Row: T. Y. Ritson (Hon. Treasurer), C. E. Foweraker, W. Dickinson, R. E. Lythgoe (Vice-President), F. Morris,
J. Kenny, R. Swindells, F. Hargreaves (Secretary).
Front Row: W. E. Bracewell, T. Laithwaite, R. Watson (Vice-President), C. E. Sutcliffe (Deputy-President), J. McKenna
(Vice-President), R. Birtwistle (Vice-President).

**MANCHESTER CITY v. SHEFFIELD UNITED.**

FIRST MATCH AT MAINE ROAD, AUGUST 25th, 1923.

L. W. Furniss (Chairman City F.C.), Max Woosnam (Captain City F.C.), The Lord Mayor of Manchester (Councillor W. Cundiff).

# CHAPTER XV.

## THE L.F.A. BENEVOLENT FUND.

*How the Fund was formed. Income and Payments. Number of cases assisted from 1919-20 to date. Contributions to the Fund from August Practice Matches receipts.*

IN the years preceding the Great War the Lancashire F.A. had many critics. It was stated, argued, and alleged that the Members of the Council were particularly out of touch with the claims of Amateur and Junior football, and there was a very determined effort to "sweep the decks."

The actual facts were that the Association had every sympathy with all kinds of organisations, whether they were Schoolboys, Juveniles, Juniors, or Intermediates, and they would have received practical help and support if there had been the funds to do so.

Likewise the Association could not venture upon a Benevolent Fund dependent upon voluntary donations. and the Association could not finance such an undertaking from its own meagre funds.

But what was not practicable up to 1914 was easy to accomplish in 1919 and onwards; the Association had become rich, the Lancashire Cup Competition had again made a great appeal to the sporting public, and it was the great success of 1919 that re-established the Association's position, and made possible the promotion of the Benevolent Fund.

The Association transferred £200 from its General Account and so commenced a Fund. that has, is, and will be, of great service to those who become ill or injured through playing football.

Each Season the Clubs are invited to contribute from their Practice Matches receipts, and they have responded right royally.

All the Senior clubs have contributed £5 or more each Season, and some of the Subscriptions were for £20, £25, £30, and £40, and on one occasion Bolton Wanderers kindly donated £100.

The Association also contributes nearly £40 per year from investments. The contributions being voluntary, it therefore follows that the payments are also voluntary, and Grants are only made in necessitous cases, and even then, only after careful enquiries by Members of the Council.

In 1919-20 10 Grants were made at a cost of £135. In 1927-28, 37 Grants were made, costing £223. No less than 314 Grants have been made since 1919, the total payments being £2,380 5s. 6d.

It will, therefore, be seen how this work has grown, and also the great financial responsibility attached to it. Not only has it been possible to assist sick and injured, players and officials, but in numerous cases where death has occurred, the needs of the widow and the orphans have been duly recognised.

Every Finance Meeting the Secretary reports grateful letters of thanks for the assistance given.

In 1927, 37 Clubs contributed £231 15s. 0d. from their Practice Matches Receipts, and whilst such splendid support is maintained, the Benevolent work of the Association will not languish.

Finally, the whole of the work is freed from working expenses, as the Association bears the cost of enquiries and administration.

During Season 1927-28 a contribution of one hundred and fifty guineas was made to the John Lewis Memorial Fund, promoted by Blackburn Rovers F.C., through which means a cot has been endowed in the East Lancashire Royal Infirmary.

## SKELMERSDALE UNITED.
### JUNIOR SHIELD WINNERS, 1907-8.

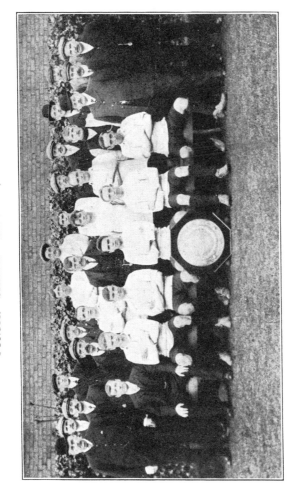

H. Ball, W. Winstanley, W. Sephton,
A. Martin, T. Brown, F. Birks, S. Dickenson,
J. Flannaghan, H. Pilkington, F. Salmon, J. Scotson, W. Dagnall.

**T. CHARNLEY.**
Hon. Auditor L.F.A.    Elected 1914.
Also Secretary, The Football League.

**A. H. DOWNS.**
Hon. Auditor L.F.A.    Elected 1904.
Also Secretary Lancashire Combination.

**W. A. DUCKWORTH.**
Member of L.F.A. Council.
1892-1918.

**J. J. HAWORTH.**
Member of L.F.A. Council.
1901-1909.

# CHAPTER XVI

## THE WORK OF THE LEAGUE'S SANCTION COMMITTEE.

*Growth of local Leagues. Model Rules formed. The work of Messrs. J. J. Haworth, J. McKenna, and E. Little. List of the oldest Leagues, etc., connected with the Association.*

The work of the Leagues Sanction Committee is probably the least known, and therefore the least appreciated by the general football public.

Prior to 1905 there was little or no control over the Rules and Regulations of Leagues, with the result that as Leagues were formed such Rules as they had, were mostly irregular, and all kinds of anomalies prevailed, and as the number of Leagues were then beginning to extend, it was fortunate that steps were taken to unify the conditions, and to make it a condition that Clubs and players should not play in any League until its Rules had been sanctioned.

The following figures indicate the growth of Leagues in Lancashire :—

In 1900 there were 9.

In 1910 there were 32.

In 1914 there were 50.

In 1919-20. First Season after the Great War, there were 40.

In 1927-28 there were 70 Leagues.

The sanction and control of 70 Leagues means that 2,000 Clubs and Teams are subject to the jurisdiction of the Association.

Leagues have to apply for renewal of sanction each Season, and that involves an enormous scrutiny of draft Rules. Some suggested copies have often been submitted in faintly written pencil, written in ink on paper like butter paper, written on both sides of the paper, or even if legibly written, the Rules themselves have been of the variety that would have puzzled " a Philadelphia lawyer."

It will, therefore, be realised how difficult the work has been, and it is no wonder that in 1905 the L.F.A. drew up a model code of Rules for the guidance and assist-ance of Leagues, and the Model Rules in force to-day are substantially the same as those first drawn up.

For a number of years the Model Rules were merely issued for the guidance of Leagues, etc., but in 1924 it was decided that all Leagues should adopt them en bloc, and that local Rules should then follow on.

Messrs. J. J. Haworth, R. Birtwistle, E. Little, A. E. Heap, D. Porteous, and J. A. MacGregor, were the Mem-bers of the first Leagues Sanction Committee, and to them, but to Mr. Haworth in particular, must be given the credit of the Model Rules which have been so essential to the sanctioning of Leagues, and have helped to minimise the difficulties, especially those of Junior organisations.

Mr. J. J. Haworth was the Leagues Sanction Chairman until 1909. Mr. J. McKenna was the next Chairman, which position he held during Season 1909-10, but in consequence of the many calls of The F.A. and of The Football League, he relinquished the position, though he continued to serve on the Committee, and in view of his extensive experience as Chairman of The F.A. Leagues Sanction Committee he has been of incalculable service.

In 1910 Mr. E. Little was appointed Chairman of the Committee, which position he still holds. If the late Mr.

J. J. Haworth laid the foundation, Mr. Little has built up the structure, and during his eighteen years as Chairman has rendered most valuable service in dealing with this great growing department of the Association. His Vice-Chairman is Mr. J. Kenny, of Preston, and the other Members of the Committee are :—

The President (Mr. C. E. Sutcliffe), Messrs. T. P. Campbell, E. Clayton, J.P., R. A. Beeley, W. Dickinson, H. Duckworth, C. E. Foweraker, H. P. Hardman, J. E. Mangnall, F. Morris, W. J. Sawyer, J. Taylor, and H Windle.

Amongst the Leagues still in existence are the following, and were first sanctioned in the years named :—

Blackburn and District Thursday League......1895.
Bolton and District A.F.A. ........................1890.
Bolton and District S.S.S. League ...............1890.
Bury and District Sunday School League ......1897.
Fylde League .....................................1898.
Lancashire Alliance ..............................1889.
Lancashire Combination ........................1891.
North Western League ..........................1900.
Oldham and District S.S. League ............1901.
Preston and District Thursday League ......1900.
Radcliffe and District Sunday School League..1899.
Ulverston and District Amateur League......1903.
West Lancashire League ........................1905.
Wigan and District S.S. League ...............1903.
Wigan and District Cup Competition .........1886.

GROUP OF PRESENT-DAY LANCASHIRE REFEREES, APPOINTED BY THE FOOTBALL LEAGUE. LEAGUE, 1928-29.

F. Hargreaves, Secretary L.F.A.; C. E. Sutcliffe, President L.F.A.; H. E. Hull (Burnley), A. Haworth (Blackpool), G. T. Davies (Bury), H. W. Norman (Preston), J. Twist, Hon. Secretary Lancashire Referees' Society. F. Robinson (Blackburn), W. F. Bunnell (Preston), A. E. Fogg (Bolton), J. Rennie (Oldham), W. E. Ryecroft (Nelson). I. Caswell (Blackburn), J. Roscoe (Bolton).

[Photo by T. S. Hargreaves, Clitheroe.]

# CHAPTER XVII.

## REFEREES.

*Registration of Referees. Examination arrangements. Some unusual answers. Lancashire Referees who have been, or are, Football League Referees. Lancashire Officials who have refereed The F.A. Cup Final.*

## LANCASHIRE FOOTBALL ASSOCIATION. REFEREES.

The problem of Referees and Refereeing is eternal, from everlasting to everlasting.

Prior to 1901 there was no registration of Referees, and the Officials were either invited by the contending Clubs, or they were asked through the Association to officiate.

Referees were selected to act without any examination, and no real system of knowing an intending Referee's abilities was in existence.

In 1901 a very definite and far reaching innovation was made. A Referees Committee was appointed whose duties were defined as follows :—

1.—To examine the qualifications of Referees.

2.—To submit applicants to such Tests theoretical or practical as they deem advisable.

3.—To report the result of all applications and enquiries, to the Lancashire F.A.

4.—To appoint Referees to matches when requested.

A further instruction stated " no Referee shall be appointed to any match in connection with any League or Competition within the area governed by the Lancashire F.A., who is not on the official Referees List of this or some other F.A. recognised by The F.A."

The Members of the first Referees Committee of the Lancashire F.A. were :—Messrs. J. Lewis, J. J. Bentley, C. E. Sutcliffe, J. S. Roscow, R. P. Gregson (Secretary), with J. T. Howcroft as Registrar.

The first list of referees contained 49 seniors and 96 juniors.

In 1910, Mr. F. Hargreaves, was appointed Registrar to the Committee, when he became the Association Secretary in 1911, and the two Offices were combined.

The Referees List has grown tremendously, there being now over 900 Referees registered by the Lancashire F.A., and in some Seasons the Lancashire List has been the largest in the Country.

Each Season about 250 candidates are examined. The examination consist of an eye sight and colour test, and a theoretical examination, part written and part oral.

Candidates for the Senior List have first to qualify for the Junior List, and they are also now required to pass a Practical Test, which means they are watched when officiating and judged accordingly.

The questions put to candidates are merely on the Laws of the Game, and are not intended as "catch" questions.

Some of the answers are worthy of mention.

" The advantages of a goalkeeper are that he can wear a cap."

Another budding knight of the whistle states " the duties of a Referee are, he must be true to his post."

The size of the goalposts are variously stated to be, " Six feet," " eight yards," and even "twelve inches," but perhaps the most ingenious reply ever given was, " I don't know, I've never measured them."

Lancashire Referees have been very successful in earning the highest honours in the game, in being appointed to officiate in Football League Matches, F.A. Cup Ties, and in International Matches.

Messrs. J. H. Alderson, D. G. Ashworth, H. Atherton, W. Atherton, A. Briggs, W. F. Bunnell, J. Butterfield, T. P. Campbell, I. Caswell, W. Chadwick, James Cooper, H. Dale, G. T. Davies, R. Eccles, L. N. Fletcher, L. W. Furniss, A. E. Fogg, W. Gilgryst, D. Hammond, A. Hargreaves, A. Haworth, T. Helme, G. Hewitt, L. P.

LANCASTER TOWN F.C.

WINNERS OF JUNIOR CUP—1927-28.

J. Livesay (Trainer), E. Fisher, R. Simms, F. Marquis, P. Floyd, W. Scott, J. P. Longworth.
H. Nicholson, J. Myerscough, H. Miller (captain), H. G. Cooper, W. Mercer.

Hitchin, H. Hopkinson, R. Holmes, J. W. Horrocks,
R. Horrocks, J. T. Howcroft, H. E. Hull, J. Kenny,
A. F. Kirby, F. Kirkham, J. Lewis, R. E. Lythgoe,
Rev. J. W. Marsh, M. McQueen, H. W. Norman,
F. T. Norreys, S. Ormerod, S. D. Peers, A. Pellowe,
J. V. Pennington, H. Pollitt, J. R. Prowse, J. Rennie,
F. Robinson, J. Roscoe, S. Rothwell, W. E. Ryecroft,
E. Shutt, L. M. Sinclair, F. Slater, J. Stott, A. F.
Sutcliffe, C. E. Sutcliffe, J. E. Telford, S. Thomas, W.
Vaughan, A. Ward, Nat. Whittaker, E. Whitehead, R.
Wild, J. E. Williams, and H. T. Yates, are all names that
one readily associates with Senior Football, all of whom
have acted, or are acting, as Football League Referees,
and also in many F.A. Cup Ties.

The following list of Lancashire Referees who have
been honoured in being appointed to referee The F.A. Cup
Final Tie is a formidable one.

1894-95.  Mr. J. Lewis (Blackburn).
1896-97.  Mr. J. Lewis (Blackburn).
1897-98.  Mr. J. Lewis (Blackburn).
1905-06.  Mr. F. Kirkham (Preston).
1906-07.  Mr. N. Whittaker (London) previously of
    Oswaldtwistle.
1907-08.  Mr. T. P. Campbell (Blackburn).
1914-15.  Mr. H. H. Taylor (Altrincham).
1919-20.  Mr. J. T. Howcroft (Bolton).
1920-21.  Mr. Job Davies (Rainhill).
1926-27.  Mr. W. F. Bunnell (Preston).

The Chairman of the L.F.A. Referees Committee is
Mr. T. Laithwaite, and the Vice-Chairman, Mr. H. Duck-
worth, and they are supported by the following Members :
Messrs. C. E. Sutcliffe (President), T. Y. Ritson, J. Taylor,
J. E. Mangnall, J. W. Walsh, R. E. Lythgoe, T. P. Camp-
bell, H. Windle, F. Morris, R. Watson, T. A. Barcroft, J.
Kenny, C. E. Foweraker, W. Dickinson, E. Clayton, J.P ,
W. J. Sawyer, E. C. Witter, J.P., most of whom have been
Referees, and are therefore appreciative of the difficulties
of Referees and Refereeing.

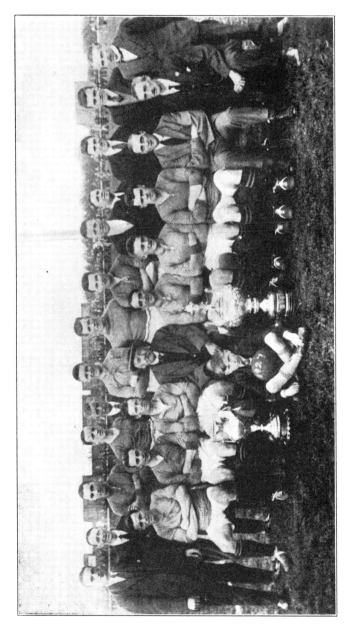

H. Gorst (Trainer), W. R. Bradbury (Secretary), F. Dickinson, J. Young, F. Bland (Director), H. Clayton, C. Clarke, J. English. G. Grass, W. B. Clarke (Director), A. Brown, N. Winn, H. Knowles.
Seated: H. Titterington, T. Ross, W. Greatorex, J. B. Christie (President), R. Carlisle (Captain), J. E. Farnworth, N. Whittaker, C. Foster, H. Rushton (Director).

**HORWICH R.M.I. F.C.**

WINNERS OF JUNIOR CUP, 1924-25.

E. Edwards (Trainer), T. Embrey, F. Blinkhorn, T. Crook, S. Gradwell, F. Walkden.

S. Embrey, G. Yates, D. Sullivan, W. Lovett (Captain), H. Croft, G. Shaw.

# CHAPTER XVIII.

## THE LANCASHIRE FOOTBALL COMBINATION.

*Formed in 1891. A Second Division added in 1903-04.*
*Withdrawal of thirteen League Clubs in 1911. Cheshire*
*Clubs also secede. Second Division abandoned. Past*
*and present Presidents and Officers. The Combination*
*a " nursery " for the higher Leagues.*

## THE LANCASHIRE FOOTBALL COMBINATION
### BY A. H. DOWNS, SECRETARY.

The Lancashire Combination was really a forced plant. There would have been no necessity for its creation had the old Lancashire League—then in its heyday—not absolutely declined to listen to the applications from the Reserve teams of League Clubs for Membership. Therefore, the League Clubs, or to be exact three of them, Blackburn Rovers, Preston North End, and Bolton Wanderers, were the chief movers in the formation of the Combination in Season 1891-92; their other Colleagues in the first Season being Hindley, Royton, North Meols, Skelmersdale United, Liverpool, Stanley, and Halliwell, all of whom, with the exception of Skelmersdale United (now in the Liverpool Combination) are names of the past, indeed Halliwell, once a noted Club, failed to complete their first Season's fixtures, and thus only eight Clubs were left at the finish. But, of course, those were the days when even The Football League had a small Membership. It may be mentioned that Blackburn Rovers Reserve won the Championship for the first three Seasons, a triple success shared only by Everton Reserve in later years.

Having made a start, the Combination progressed by leaps and bounds, so much so that in Season 1903-04 a

Second Division was instituted, but this was discontinued at the end of Season 1914-15. Of course the Combination was primarily for the benefit of League Clubs, and with a view to stimulating the non-League Clubs a Member of the Committee, Mr. R. Watson, induced the President of Accrington Stanley, Captain Harwood, J.P., in Season 1902-03 to present a set of medals for the non-League Club securing the highest position in the table. Singularly his own Club, Accrington Stanley, that year established a record by becoming the first non-League Club to win the Championship, so that they actually secured two sets of medals for the feat. Mr. J. McKenna and Mr. C. E. Sutcliffe also offered medals for the two following Seasons, when it was felt that the two classes of Members were more on an equal footing.

But before the two Division stage had been reached much spade work had to be done. The first big change came about when in Season 1894-95 there was an amalgamation with the North-East Lancashire League, and also the introduction of the Reserve teams of such Clubs as Everton, Burnley, Manchester City, and Newton Heath (the latter were, of course, the forerunners of Manchester United, and it may be added that the Ardwick first team played in the Combination before being known as Manchester City). Most important of all, along with the North-East Lancashire League came the personality of Mr. C. E. Sutcliffe, who was Secretary of the Combination for the next four Seasons. It is not too much to say that Mr. Sutcliffe was the guiding light of the Combination for a long period, just as he is at the present time of The Football League, the Lancashire Football Association, and in no small degree of The Football Association. His legislative genius, in the football sense of course, was really grounded in the Combination. At the time of the amalgamation with his old League, he re-wrote the Rules of the Combination, and it is striking testimony to his aforesight that in the main they remain as drafted by him with very little alteration to this day. In due course Mr. Sutcliffe took his place as a Member of the Management Committee, later he was appointed President, but his term of the latter office was of very short duration owing to some slight disagreement, and he is now a Member of the Board of Appeal, so that he has had thirty-three years association with the Combination. The old Lancashire League was gradually declining, for the reason that its Members slowly but surely preferred to be associated with the limelight of Football League Clubs. In conjunction with the late Mr. Harry Hamer, of Bury, Mr. Sutcliffe arranged with his Colleagues that the Lancashire League should come bodily into the fold, and to this day the title of the Combination is " the Lancashire Football Combination, with which is incorporated the Lancashire League.

The ex-Lancashire League Clubs also brought in their handsome Cup, and this was put up for Competition by the newly formed Second Division Clubs in Season 1903-04, of which Southport Central were the first winners. The old Lancashire League had undoubtedly raised the standard of football in the County, and such Clubs as Liverpool, Bury, and Blackpool,, are striking products.

So far the Combination had recorded steadfast progress, but a period came when the whole of the thirteen League Clubs withdrew their Membership. This drastic step, taken at the Annual Meeting in 1911, came as a shock, and they were pressed to re-consider their decision. They were adamant, however, and there came into being The Central League, which is now a great power in the Football World.

The Combination rallied, but a few Seasons later the Cheshire Clubs also seceded, to form the Cheshire County League, and then came more withdrawals when the Third Division of The Football League was established. Therefore it may be claimed, and not without some pride, that the Lancashire Combination provided the backbone of three new Leagues, which have been most successful. Of course this meant a gradual weakening of the Combination, and at the end of 1914-15 the Second Division had to be abandoned with hope of a renewal at the close of the

War, but these hopes have not been gratified  simply because of the fact that the populous centres have been so
drained that with few exceptions only very Junior Clubs
are now available for Membership of a possible Second
Division.

However, it may be said that the Lancashire Combination is now a Combination of Lancashire Clubs (which
is as it should be) and recognised as the official League of
the County, to which all Lancashire Clubs aspire.    There
are some at the Manchester  end,  like  Hurst,  Ashton
National, Manchester North End,  and  Eccles  United,
whom we would like to see back in the Combination, but
these Clubs prefer to play in the Cheshire County League
as a matter of convenience.

Again, the Lancashire Combination has been managed
by men who have occupied high positions in the legislative world.   The first President was Mr. T. Heaton, of
Burnley.    Then followed Mr.  J.  McKenna, who had a
long spell of office.   After the " split " Mr. Sutcliffe took
charge for a few months, and on his resignation the late
Mr. J. Lewis was approached  and  promised  to  accept
office for one Season, just to pull the Combination together
as it were, and then to retire on account of his numerous
appointments in connection with Football, and other organisations.   But he was not allowed to get away so easily,
and as a matter of fact he continued in office until his
death, when he was succeeded by the present President,
Mr. T. P. Campbell, who may be  said  to  have  been
" schooled " by his fellow townsman.   But as I have said
the Combination has ever been managed by men of dis-
cernment.   Men like Messrs. J. McKenna, C. E. Sutcliffe,
the late J. J. Bentley, and the late J. Lewis, are names
that stand out in the history of the Game.    Then there
were the late H. S. Hamer, the late T. Houghton, J. T.
Howcroft, F. Kirkham, and many others, whilst two of
the present Committeemen, Messrs. R. Watson and W.
Knowles are worthy of special mention, for each has spent
over 20 years in Combination work.   Like the President,

Mr. R. Watson, is a valued Member of the Council of the Lancashire Football Association, as are also Messrs. R. A. Beeley and E. Clayton. Mr. C. Holgate has also had a lifelong connection with the game. The writer has been officially connected with the Combination since its inception. First a Member of the Committee, later became Treasurer, and on the resignation of Mr. Sutcliffe from the post of Secretary in 1898 was elected to succeed him.

No fewer than nine of the present Northern Section of the Third Division of The Football League are old Members of the Combination, and of the present Members Chorley have perhaps maintained the most consistent record, both in the Combination and in the Lancashire Junior Cup Competition. Lancaster Town have also had a very satisfactory experience, whilst Darwen, though having done well on the whole, have not been fortunate in securing honours. Of recent years Morecambe have also been very prominent.

# CHAPTER XIX.

## LANCASHIRE F.A. AND THE GREAT WAR.

*Condition of L.F.A. and prospects in August, 1914. The Call to Arms. Appeal to Clubs. Help for the War Fund. Enlistment of Lancashire Footballers. Early Casualties. War Time Football. Letters from the Trenches. Football Talk, Optimism and Patriotism.*

WHEN the War was declared on that memorable 4th August, 1914, the Lancashire F.A. was in a most flourishing condition, and the prospects for Season 1914-15 pointed to a record Season, but the call to arms altered everything. Many Leagues cancelled their arrangements, scores of Clubs announced that they had suspended operations, in some cases whole teams enlisted together, and yet again such organisations as could carry on, immediately arranged matches for War Funds, comforts for the troops, etc.

The F.A. issued a circular appealing "to the patriotism of all who are interested in the game to support the Nation in the present serious emergency . . . Players and spectators who are physically fit and otherwise able are urged to join the Army at once." On 2nd September, 1914, the Lancashire F.A. met to consider the situation, needless to state it approved and commended The F.A. appeal, and it further voted £100 to the Prince of Wales War Fund. The Lancashire F.A. also suggested to its Clubs the advisability of throwing open their grounds for military training, further the Clubs were requested to have extended half-time intervals, so that Recruiting addresses could be delivered.

Within a month of the outbreak of War £1,733 was raised by Lancashire Clubs for the War Fund. Appeals for football outfits for matches which were actually played behind the lines " were constantly made, and the response was gratifying and cheering. The ball used in the Junior Cup Final Tie, played 27th March, 1915, was sent to the 5th Battalion The King's Own Royal Regiment.

Up to Conscription being adopted an attempt was made to record the enlistment of Lancashire footballers, which list gave a total of 4,765 who had enlisted in the Army or Navy, the recruits having been connected with the following organisations :—

Amateur Clubs (9 clubs) ........................... 473
Barrow Thursday League ........................... 18
Blackburn Thursday League ..................... 40
Blackburn and District Sunday School League 133
Blackburn and District Combination ......... 357
Bolton Wednesday League ........................ 54
Bolton Sunday School Social League ......... 297
Bolton and District A.F.A. ........................ 117
Burnley and District Tuesday League ......... 18
Burnley and District Amateur League ......... 64
Bury and District Sunday School League ... 204
Bury and District Amateur League .............. 174
Bury Junior League ................................. 144
Colne and District Sunday School League ... 101
Darwen and District Sunday School League... 54
Farnworth and District Amateur League ...... 107
Rossendale and District F.A. (8 clubs) ......... 40
Football League (11 clubs) ........................ 40
Fylde Wednesday League ........................ 119
Hooley Hill and District Sunday School
　League ............................................... 83
Lancashire Combination (17 clubs) ............ 186
Lancashire and Cheshire League (5 clubs) ... 100
Leigh and District Sunday School League... 165
Lune District F.A. .................................... 246
North Western League ............................. 65
Oswaldtwistle and District Sunday School
　League ............................................... 70
Preston and District Thursday League (6 clubs) 46
Preston and District Amateur League (6 clubs) 80
Radcliffe and District Sunday School League 305

Rossendale and District Sunday School
    League ................................................ 37
Rossendale and District F.A. (about 8 clubs)  40
Ulverston and District League  .................. 136
West Lancashire League  ........................... 280
Wigan and District Combination  ..............  63
Registered Referees  ...............................  48
Others not Classified  .............................. 301

                                    ———
                    Grand Total  ...............4765
                                    ———

Amongst the early casualties was Lieutenant R. E.
Weigall, of the Sherwood Foresters, who was killed in
action at Neuve Chapelle.   He was Secretary of his team
for two Seasons whilst stationed at Fleetwood, and G. V.
Buxton, of Bury, a most promising Senior Referee, also
made the great sacrifice in July, 1915, and later " Eddie "
Latheron, of Blackburn Rovers, was also numbered
amongst the " honoured dead."

Many Clubs lost some of their brightest and best
players, such as E. Hodgson, Burnley, and Edward Bullen,
Bury.

Season 1915-16 saw football so transformed as to be
almost unrecognisable.   The F.A. Cup, the Lancashire
Cup, and other Lancashire Competitions, dropped.   The
League Clubs grouped into convenient geographical groups,
and no payment of players.  Did football so played justify
its continuance ? It did. It heartened the men at the "front,"
it gave them something to think, talk, and argue about, it
helped those who had to stay at home, and when the boys
had a " blighty " how they turned up at these improvised
games, and how they enjoyed them.

A few quotations from letters received may be of interest.

" I shall come home on the last boat that leaves France
after victory has been won.  We must win, and we are resolved to win no matter what the cost may be."   That is
a quotation from a Footballer, 23 years of age, after having spent two years in the fighting line.

Another player (somewhere in Belgium) a mid-week League player, wrote, "You can take it from us that "strafing" the Hun is much more exciting than kicking the winning goal in a Cup Final. We recently met a few of the Blackburn Thursday League players, and we did not forget to bring the good old football topic on the carpet."

I. Caswell, now a Football League Referee, wrote, "I see the good old Rovers won on Saturday, and it was pleasing to us here. There are three or four Blackburn men here, and very often on Saturday's we talk about Ewood Park, and as there are boys from other Lancashire towns we have many football arguments. We are all well and feeling ready for Fritz."

Yet another wrote home to an anti-conscriptionist. "Throw away your principles man, throw away the limber of the past, and look things in the face. Don't bother about God upholding the cause of the just, and that bull dog pluck will pull us through—I am tired of pulpit and music hall sentiments. Try to teach your vast masses of British opinion to surpass the Germans at their own game."

And so one could quote by the score the stirring messages from men facing death. The manhood of Lancashire (as of every other County) rallied to the assistance of England and humanity, and the great game of War was played and fought until victory was secured. The 23rd Battalion of the Middlesex Regiment was known as the Footballers Battalion, and many Lancashire players served in it with great distinction.

The Great War, with its great world upheaval only seems now an ugly nightmare, yet there are some things that remind us of its terrible reality, i.e. the loss of those who made the "supreme sacrifice."

When the Armistice was declared and Peace ensured, it needed no stimulation to arouse a Football public, the boys spared to come home, having served their King and Country, turned naturally to the king of games, and within an incredibly short period Clubs and Leagues were again assembled, and Football enjoyed a wonderful boom.

# CHAPTER XX.

## PROFESSIONALISM IN FOOTBALL.

### HOW LANCASHIRE FORCED ITS LEGALISATION.

*Professionalism in Football. How Lancashire forced its legalisation.*

By J. K. FLETCHER
(*Olympian*" of the "*Bolton Evening News.*")

It is a true saying that what Lancashire does and says to-day, England does and says to-morrow. England would have nothing to do with professional football until the shrewd, hard-headed committee-men who were responsible for the control of Lancashire clubs made up their minds that, if the Soccer game was to prosper and strengthen its hold on the sporting public, the payment of players must be legalised.

In the early eighties, when Scottish players were imported, it was quickly realised that they could not be regarded as strict amateurs, for men would not leave their homes to assist a club in which they had no interest, at a town in which they had no friends, unless they were well paid; and the Lancashire clubs came to the conclusion that it would be far better to acknowledge professional players than to encourage the deception which was rife.

They saw no reason why football should be regarded as a strictly amateur game. There were, they argued, professionals in every class of sport, many of whom were just as much respected as those who played for enjoyment

**J. YATES.**
Burnley F.C.

**J. W. CRABTREE.**
Burnley F.C. and Aston Villa F.C.

**W. BANNISTER.**
Burnley F.C. and Bolton Wanderers F.C.

**J. REYNOLDS.**
West Bromwich Albion F.C. and
Aston Villa F.C.

[Photos of Crabtree and Reynolds by A. Wilkes, Birmingham.]

alone, and so rather than go on acting in defiance of the laws of The Football Association, they resolved to force the governing body to legalise professionalism.

The Association were just as determined that professionalism and importation of players should not be permitted, and a new set of Cup rules, framed so as to leave no loophole, were sent out to the clubs, who were ordered to submit names of all players of different nationality to the club, or imported from any other district, together with the wages such players were receiving, and the amount they received at their previous residence. Clubs not under suspicion were forbidden to play clubs who were suspect.

Thus was the gauntlet thrown down, and the Lancashire clubs promptly accepted the challenge. Nine of them sent representatives to a meeting at the Commercial Hotel, Bolton, on Friday, October 10th, 1884, and what could have been more appropriate than that they should appoint Mr. W. Sudell, who brought together Preston North End's team that became known as the Old Invincibles, as chairman. Other Clubs represented were Astley Bridge, Bolton Wanderers, Burnley, Burnley Union Star, Great Lever, Halliwell, Padiham and Preston Zingari.

This meeting was adjourned until the following Wednesday at the Bay Horse Hotel, Blackburn, when, in addition to the original nine clubs, Accrington, Blackburn Park Road, Bolton Association, Church, Clitheroe, Peel Bank Rovers, Rawtenstall, and Turton, were represented. The original minute Book states that seven of the clubs decided to withdraw from The F.A. Cup Competition, and that all clubs not taking part in it should refuse to fill up the form sent out by The F.A. on the ground that the latter had no right to require the registration of players for matches other than those of the Cup Competition.

Realising that if they were loyal to each other, they could defy the authorities, the Lancashire clubs formed the British National Association, to embrace clubs and players of every nationality, and they promptly called a conference of clubs at Manchester, where seventy clubs were represented including Aston Villa and Sunderland, and a deputation was appointed to meet the Lancashire F.A. Committee in a conference at which Mr. R. P. Gregson was empowered to attend the next meeting of The Football Association in London, and move an amendment to the rule which sought to interfere with ordinary club fixtures.

By this time The Football Association began to recognise the force of the opposition. The spread of professionalism to the Midlands strengthened Lancashire's case, and early in November, 1884, they appointed a sub-committee to consider the whole question, and as a consequence of the report which the sub-committee presented, The Football Association on December 1st, 1884, to the complete satisfaction of the Lancashire clubs, whose determined attitude was completely vindicated, not only recommended the legalisation of professionals, but also suggested that professionals should be allowed to compete for the cup.

The matter was put to the vote at a meeting in London on January 19th, 1885, and amongst those who spoke in favour of professionalism being legalised was Mr. Gregson, for many years the Secretary of the Lancashire Association, who confessed that his Association had tried their best to stamp out professionalism, but had not succeeded. In spite of that, there voted for professionalism 113, against 108, so that it did not get the requisite two thirds majority, and was declared lost.

Then came a lull. The Association Committee for some time did nothing to discourage professionalism, which continued on the increase. On the contrary players were selected for International honours, who, if not openly acknowledged as professionals, were under suspicion of receiving remuneration for their services in connection with the game.

On March 23rd, 1885, a further meeting of The Football Association took place at Anderton's Hotel, London, at which Mr. Gregson's proposal that professionalism be legalised was received with great cheering, but though supported by 106 votes to 69, the two-thirds majority was still not forthcoming. Before the meeting dispersed, however, a sub-committee was appointed to consider the question with a view to affecting a compromise.

The report of this sub-committee expressed the opinion that it was now expedient, in the interests of Association football to legalise the employment of professional football players under certain restrictions. This report was considered by The Football Association at a meeting on July 20th, 1885, when 35 of the 47 people present voted for the adoption of the report and only five against.

Lancashire's representatives at that final epoch-making gathering were Dr. Morley (Blackburn Rovers), Messrs. T. Hindle (Darwen), A. Kent (Darwen Old Wanderers), J. J. Bentley (Bolton Wanderers), and Mr. R. P. Gregson (Secretary of the Lancashire F.A.), names that are still revered in football circles for the part they played in legalising the payment of players. But even they could not have foreseen the far reaching effects of the stand they took or the gigantic strides the game has since made in public favour.

**H. JONES.**
Blackburn Rovers F.C.

**H. MAKEPEACE.**
Everton F.C.

**J. HOLT.**
Everton F.C. and Reading F.C.

**E. CHADWICK.**
Everton F.C.

# CHAPTER XXI.

## LANCASHIRE F.A. AND THE FIGHT FOR PROFESSIONALISM.

*Extracts from Minutes. Quotations from N. L. Jackson's " Association Football." The Rovers and " Jimmie" Costley. Upton Park protest against Preston North End on the grounds of professionalism.*

OCTOBER 12TH, 1882.

" A representative of " Manchester Courier " having written the Secretary (Mr. R. P. Gregson) asking for information respecting professionals playing in Lancashire teams, the Secretary was instructed to reply to the effect that this Committee has no official knowledge of professionals playing in Lancashire teams, but that if evidence of the playing of professionals could be brought forward they were prepared to take the matter up."

NOVEMBER 1ST, 1882.

" A letter from Birmingham Association protesting against continual importation of foreign players into Lancashire clubs and refusing to play against them in the match, Lancashire v. Birmingham, on November 25th, the Secretary was instructed to reply stating that it was the intention of the Committee to select only those players who are eligible to play for the Lancashire Cup under our own Rules."

The only qualification at that period was having been a recognised playing member of a club for twenty-eight days.

NOVEMBER 24TH, 1882.

"A letter from Sheffield Association received, objecting to play against " other than bona-fide Lancashire men."

The following extracts from L. N. Jackson's book, " Association Football," are very illuminating.

" Very early in the Season the Birmingham Association entered the lists against professionalism and disqualified A. Jones (Walsall), D. Hodgetts and Green (St. George's), for

having received payment for playing in Lancashire. Shortly
afterwards a Lancashire paper published a letter signed by
J. Costley, a member of the Blackburn  Olympic  Club,
stating, ``that he had met J. Lewis (late Secretary of the
Blackburn Rovers' Club) and W. Duckworth by appointment, when they promised, if he would join the Rovers, to
give him a share of the gate-money of the Notts County
match, and told him that he would be almost sure of International and County honours, as they had such influence
on the English and Lancashire Committees.'' This, and
many other occurrences. demonstrated to a certainty that
the evasion of the amateur laws was the rule rather than
the exception in certain districts, and at last The Football
Association was forced to take action.   The first con-
viction was at the instance of the Darwen Club (which was
probably the pioneer of veiled professionalism), and  the
offenders were  a  player  named  Beresford  and  the
Accrington Club.  The former was declared to be a professional, and  the  latter  was  expelled  from  the
Association.''

    `` Early in 1884 the Upton Park Club protested against
Preston North End on the grounds of professionalism. The
case came before a special and largely attended meeting
of the committee held at Kennington Oval. The scene was
one not likely to be forgotten.  Hitherto it had been almost
impossible to convict offending clubs because of the tacit
conspiracy which existed to prevent the facts from coming
to the knowledge of the committee.  On this occasion Mr.
Sudell, the President of the Preston North End Club, and
practically the manager of it, was called before the committee. and, instead of avoiding the issue, he caused in-
tense astonishment by admitting at once that they paid their
players, and added that he could prove that nearly every
other important club in Lancashire and in the Midlands did
the same.    After this admission the committee had  no
other alternative but to disqualify the Preston Club.  No
further steps were taken then, because it was felt that after
such a frank confession the matter must be dealt with by
the Association.''

**LANCASHIRE F.A. OFFICES,**
42, ST. GEORGE'S PLACE, BLACKBURN.

# CHAPTER XXII.

## BIOGRAPHIES.

In presenting the following biographies of men who came into football when it was in its infancy, it necessarily follows that incidents connected with the growth and development of the game must be included, indeed, the recital of some of the incidents probably portray their characteristics much better than the mere use of phrases, however appreciative the latter may be used.

The year 1918 was a a memorable one for the Lancashire F.A., the following members all " passing the bar," R. P. Gregson—who had retired in 1911—died in April, J. S. Roscow in August, J. J. Bentley in September, and the then President of the Association, D. B. Woolfall in October, and also W. A. Duckworth, who represented Division Four, also died that month.

These losses were a severe blow to the Association, and the L.F.A. received messages of sympathy from all parts of the Country.

The following pages are dedicated to the memory of the men who did so much in the early days to establish our game and to administer its rules, and at the same time to show the different parts they played in the changes that took place.

## JOHN LEWIS.

### By Mr. C. E. Sutcliffe.

Born at Market Drayton on 30th March, 1855, died at Blackburn, 13th January, 1926. Member of the Council from 1889, elected Vice-President on 12th June, 1901, and President after the death of Mr. D. B. Woolfall on 8th November, 1918. His life was full of enthusiasm for the game, and he practically died in harness.

He was one of the founders and pioneers of Blackburn Rovers Club in connection with which Club he was Treasurer from 1881 to 1894, and was a member of the Committee until 1897. As a referee he stood in the front rank, not so much because either players or Clubs loved him as that all feared him. He knew the Laws of the Game from beginning to end, and his keen eye detected all the tricks of the players. Ready and stern to punish, everybody knew he would stand no nonsense, and visiting Clubs could rely on him to discharge his duties fearlessly, hence they got a square deal. As a referee he stood at the top, yet he was always willing to help any other referee, not merely to understand the Laws of the Game, but to adopt the best methods of control. His criticism was often severe, but that was his method of teaching referees to be honest and strong.

His honesty in all his work has never been doubted, and when Mr. Woolfall was laid to rest, Mr. Lewis was the only man whose claims to the Presidency could be considered. He was so enthusiastic that he made a hobby of all his work in football. For years he must have been one of the best known men on the Railway, for not only was he prepared to referee football matches anywhere and at any time, but addresses on Football Sundays and Referees Meetings specially appealed to him. He never claimed to be an orator, but he had always a definite message to deliver, which he did in plain homely fashion and feared no man.

L

He loved his work and was particularly proud of the
positions he held in connection with the The Football Association, the Football League, and the Lancashire Football
Association, and he was very happy in doing all he could
to further the game amongst the Junior Clubs.  He was a
born fighter, gloried in argument, was persistent in maintaining his view, and generally succeeded in getting his
way.  He carried his strict methods of refereeing into all
phases of his work.  Only his closest friends understood him. for he was so obsessed with his own ideas,
so convinced that his judgment was always right, and had
so little sympathy with anyone who did not act  as  he
thought they ought; that he was at times a stormy petrel
and never hesitated to attack, in what seemed to many of
us the most savage and violent fashion, some  of his best
friends.  He made friends innumerable, for he was at the
call of all.  We loved him as President because he had
always in mind what was best for the game.  He has fallen
foul of most of us, and we have been astounded at what
seemed the bitterness of his attacks, but we soon learnt
that his bark was worse than his bite, that his severe regard
for what seemed to him to be the honest course for a time
subdued his merciful judgment, but in the end his better
nature rose to the top and just as he never harboured ill
will towards any of us we could feel no ill against him.

As a pioneer of the game it was fitting that he should
become a missionary for football, and not only through
Great Britain and Ireland, but on the Continent, and away
in South Africa and Australia, he will be ever remembered
for the vast contribution he made to the  game  in  all  its
phases.  What the sacrifice of home life and comforts,
coupled with the strain of constant and wearying travel
during the trips to South Africa and Australia meant to him,
none can tell ; those who made the journey agree that
he never spared himself, but threw his heart and soul in his
work, devoting time and money to a ceaseless propaganda
in our Colonies where football was in its infancy. Whilst in
Australia it fell to my lot to act as his Deputy, and on his
return he took hold of the work without a scrap of arrears

to deal with. Had it been true of all his other offices, he would have been saved much of the worry and anxiety which beset him on his return.

He had his failings, but we admired him none the less for that. At times too hasty in jumping to conclusions and too prone to regard a rumour as true, and guilt before proof had been tendered, there was a danger of him doing the very thing he prided himself that he would never do, that was to act unfairly.

There were times when I almost felt that he went out of his way to interfere with matters that did not concern him, and it became necessary for someone to act as peacemaker. Occasionally he conceived some new idea and with so much faith in himself he believed in its serviceability. At times it might have been better had he exercised a greater patience before committing himself and taken counsel of others, but we have far greater failings, and may be have far less reasons to criticise, still I crave compassion the more so, because I believe with all his failings he was one of the greatest men that ever took part in the conduct, control, and government of the game.

Let us remember that honesty is not the outcome of leniency. Friendship calls for honesty rather than favour. His name is honoured and his memory respected throughout the land, and the present home of the Lancashire Football Association, which he formally opened on January 29th, 1925, will stand as a lasting memorial to the memory of John Lewis.

## D. B. WOOLFALL.

Mr. Woolfall had a long and close connection with football. Originally he was associated with Blackburn Rovers, and served on the Committee for some time, but was not a playing member of the famous club.

Mr. Woolfall first joined the Lancashire F.A. in 1881, and took his share of work during the anxious and troublesome period of the early "eighties." In May, 1901, he was elected President in succession to the late Mr. W. Forrest.

Mr. Woolfall was Hon. Treasurer of The F.A. to which position he was appointed in 1900.  He was also President of the Federation Internationale de Football Association instituted at Paris in May, 1904.  Mr. Woolfall was also on the International Selection Committee, but his best work was that of a financial expert in dealing with The F.A. Accounts, and in helping to build up the financial strength of The Association.  In his younger days he was Secretary of the East Lancashire Cricket Club.

When Mr. Woolfall passed away on the 24th October, 1918, Lancashire football lost a member who by his dignity and his sincerity had done much to raise the standard of the game.

## T.  HINDLE.

Mr. T. Hindle played with Darwen F.C., but an accident terminated his playing days.  He then turned enthusiastically to the administrative side of the game.

Mr. Hindle was one of the founders of the Lancashire F.A. and was Secretary from its inception until he retired in 1882, but was then appointed Hon. Treasurer, which position he held until May, 1915.  When the legalisation of professionalism was first mooted Mr. Hindle was very hostile to the new proposal, and, indeed, he always regretted the adoption of professionalism.

In different chapters of this History there are extracts from Minutes and other references which indicate not only the work of Mr. Hindle, but as Pioneer Secretary of the Association, also disclose some of the difficulties he had to contend with.

Whatever may be the future of the Association, the name of Thomas Hindle must always be remembered in appreciation of his great work in assisting in the foundation of the Association and in building it up, notwithstanding all the turmoil and strife which reigned during the early days of the organisation.

# CHAPTER XXIII.

## BIOGRAPHIES—*continued*.

### J. S. ROSCOW.

John Roscow was one of the pioneers of football. Although quiet and unassuming, he had the courage of his convictions, he was not a platform man, but he was none the less a great worker, dour and determined, to cleanse football from anything discreditable. During his thirty-four years in connection with the Lancashire F.A. Mr. Roscow travelled thousands of miles in his attendance at Meetings.

Mr. Roscow was induced to take an active part in football in a very curious manner. He was in the seventies a follower of Rugby football, but he was prevailed upon to go and watch an Association match between Great Lever and Turton, on the ground near Doe Hey Reservoir, but it was not a pleasant experience or introduction to the game in which later Mr. Roscow was going to play a big part. "I was never more disgusted in my life," once declared Mr. Roscow when referring to this match, and he added, "the language was so abominable that I left the ground before half-time." A few days later Mr. Roscow was asked to become a Member of the Great Lever Committee. At first he declined, stating that he had heard more bad language at their match than he had heard for a long time, and the deputation replied they were seeking his help so as to help them to stop it. So Mr. Roscow became a Committeeman of Great Lever F.C., and was Secretary from 1880 to 1886.

In 1881-82 Great Lever had a curious experience in the Lancashire Cup Competition, for after defeating Eagley and Liverpool they were drawn against Irwell Springs, and

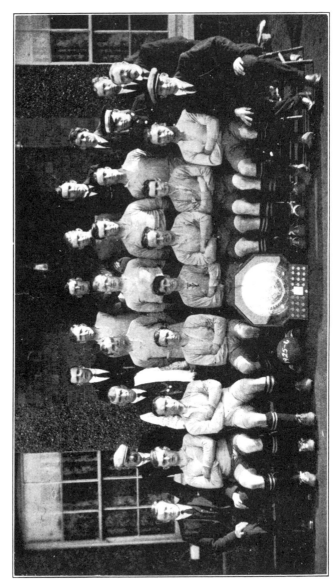

## WESTHOUGHTON COLLIERY F.C.
### WINNERS OF JUNIOR SHIELD, 1925-26.

Back Row: W. Silcock (Chairman), W. Rothwell, J. Simm, R. Davies, J. Farrimond (Secretary).
Middle Row: T. Whittingham (Trainer), J. Settle, W. Thomasson, H. Crompton, F. Preston.
Front Row: A. Latham, S. Embrey, J. Jones, W. Chadwick, J. Fairhurst, H. Ralphs, J. Wilkinson.

met them three times. Owing to a difficulty arising over George Sharples, whose qualification was impugned, they however survived the round, but were thrown out of the Competition by Blackburn Olympic.. On another occasion Great Lever went to play Lockwood Brothers at Sheffield, and to Mr. Roscow's chagrin his team were down by three goals at half-time, and he spoke to the players, telling them "they were making a mess of things." Dennis Hodgetts—who was playing for Great Lever—assured Mr. Roscow that they would win, but the latter retorted, "I'd sooner see it than hear it," but win they did, for they scored nine times in the second half. and their opponents did not score again.

Mr. Roscow was concerned in the introduction of professionalism. The paying of players had become a scandal in 1884, and The F.A. took the matter up and circularised the Clubs, as a result of which some Clubs refused to play others. This left Great Lever without a match, and Mr. Stephen Tillotson, who was a Member of the Lancashire F.A., and also a Member of Burnley F.C., tried to arrange a match with Mr. Roscow, and arising out of their conversation it was decided to take steps to call a meeting, and at Mr. Roscow's suggestion Mr. Tillotson went to see Mr. Sudell, of Preston North End, and the latter decided such meeting should be held in Bolton. The following extract from the Minutes of such meeting, recorded in the handwriting of Mr. W. Sudell is interesting :—

" Meeting of football representatives held at the Commercial Hotel, Bolton, on Friday, 10th October, 1884, at 7 p.m. Present: Mr. Sudell (North End), in the Chair, Moore and McGregor (Zingari), Roscow, Helme, and Hardy (Great Lever), Brownlow and Pendlebury (Halliwell), Leech, Bradshaw and Tillotson (Burnley), W. Taylor (Bolton Wanderers), Whittaker (Burnley Union Star), Walmsley (Padiham), Sleigh, Gregory, and Mallison (Astley Bridge).

Mr. Sudell explained the action taken by the National Football Association in the matter of imported players. A question was asked whether, in the event of Great Lever playing Burnley on the morrow, the Clubs present would support them. As neither of the Clubs were in the Cup Competition the opinion appeared to be that the Association would have no jurisdiction in this particular case. The two Clubs, however, agreed to play the match entirely on their own responsibility, the meeting declining to commit itself.

Resolved—That a meeting of the representatives of the Clubs present, and those named below, be called to consider the requirements of the Association, the meeting to be held at the Bay Horse, Blackburn, on Wednesday : Accrington, Blackburn Park Road., Rawtenstall, Blackburn, Clitheroe, Low Moor and Witton.

This was the forerunner of other meetings, and ultimately The F.A., after a strong fight to maintain Amateurism, had to capitulate to opinion that had rapidly gained ground since the question was openly mooted.

Mr. Roscow discovered some players who became famous, amongst these being Johnny Goodall, the prince of centre-forwards, and Jimmy Trainer, as fine a goalkeeper as ever played between the posts.

Mr. Roscow was one of the first League Referees, and took his last match in October, 1896. He often told the writer the reason of his retirement from refereeing, it was in his own words, " because in one match I tried to please both sides, I pleased neither, and I displeased myself."

As Chairman of the Discipline Committee he was constant in attendance, and great was his righteous indignation when dealing with youths reported for the use of obscene and dirty language. " Would you like your mother to hear such talk," he once asked a youthful offender. The reply was a flood of tears. The boy's mother had only recently died, and Mr. Roscow's shot had touched a sore spot.

Many times he would advise those guilty of using foul language " to climb a hill, as far away from anybody as you can get, and shout your dirty talk, and see if you are not ashamed of its sound."

Mr. Roscow gave devoted and loyal service to the Lancashire F.A., and from 1884 to 1905 he only missed three meetings of the Association, and in the latter years of his life, when the Discipline Committee were dealing with an average of 500 cases each Season, he was attending 60 meetings a year. Mr. Roscow was also a very keen " Wanderer " and was a life Member of the Club.

Mr. Roscow died on 6th August, 1918, in his 77th year, and singular to relate the present Secretary of the Lancashire F.A. was at the door of his residence ringing for admission at the very moment the old veteran was changing mortality for immortality.

Mr. Roscow was a Vice-President of the Association, and he held a Long Service Medal, in addition to which he held many offices in connection with Bolton and district football organisations.

## J. J. BENTLEY.

The death of J. J. Bentley took place at Fairhaven on the 2nd September, 1918, and so one more link with early time football was severed.

In his early 'teens he played for Turton, the oldest known Club in Lancashire. Those were the days when J. C. Kay and W. T. Dixon, of Turton, J. Lewis and R. Birtwistle, of Blackburn, and T. Hindle, of Darwen, were endeavouring to establish organised Association football. In 1880-81-82, Mr. Bentley was the Captain of Turton F.C., and he won his County Caps by playing as inside-right for Lancashire against Cheshire and Staffordshire.

It was at Turton that J. J. Bentley had his first insight into club management, being Hon. Secretary and Treasurer. From Turton he went to Bolton, and it was there whilst working as an Accountant that he acted in his spare time as Secretary to the Bolton Wanderers F.C., of which Club he became Chairman ten years later.

Mr. Bentley was one of the founders of The Football League, and in 1893 became the President, which position he held until 1910, when he was elected a Life Member of the League. When the late T. Hindle resigned the Secretaryship of Lancashire F.A. in 1882, there was keen competition for the post, and Mr. Bentley was one of the applicants, in fact he was one of the last two to be voted upon, but the late R. P. Gregson was the successful candidate.

J. J. Bentley also became a Vice-President of The F.A., he joined the Lancashire F.A. in 1887, and was made a Vice-President on 12th June, 1901. He, of course, held the L.F.A. Long Service Medal which he received in 1908, he also held long service medals of The F.A. and of The Football League. Not only had J. J. Bentley a large experience in the management of Leagues and Clubs, but his journalistic work was well known, widely read and closely followed by the football reading public.

His life began in Turton, being born there in 1860, and his football activities began there. It was, therefore, fitting that he should be laid to rest in the village of his birth, and the place that gave birth to organised football. When the large assembly of football representatives met at Turton on the 5th September, 1918, the Great War was still raging, and yet how peaceful was the country side. Football was then in a very low state consequent upon the call for men to serve their King and Country, but the end of the War was within sight.

J. J. Bentley had fought his fight, his battles were over, and representatives of football organisations, great and small, far and near, gathered to pay homage to him. his memory, and his work.

## CHAPTER XXIV.

### BIOGRAPHIES—*continued*.

### THE LATE R. P. GREGSON.

Mr. Gregson was elected Secretary of the Lancashire F.A. in 1882, the appointment then being merely a part time one, and he not only did great work for Lancashire F.A., but he carried numerous proposals which revolutionised the methods of The F.A.

He headed an agitation in favour of the legalisation of professionalism, and though defeated in his first attempt, he continued the campaign until success crowned his efforts. Mr. Gregson also secured more representation of the North on The F.A., the President and Secretary of that body resigning as a protest, but eventually harmony was restored. A scheme drawn up by Mr. Gregson and Mr. D. B. Woolfall, was accepted, whereby there was a re-distribution of seats. From that event evolved the division of the area of The F.A. and divisional elections.

The system of a qualifying Competition also emanated in the brain of Mr. Gregson.

R. P. Gregson, or " Dick," as he was known to his friends, was a Member of The F.A. Council until 1911, and during that long connection was a Member of most important Committees, giving particular service on the International Selection Committee. At one period he was one of the best known of Referees, and officiated in many F.A.

**R. KELLY.**
Huddersfield Town F.C.

**L. A. PAGE.**
Burnley F.C.

**W. WATSON.**
Burnley F.C

**J. DAWSON.**
Burnley F.C.

Cup Ties, Scottish Cup Ties, and International Matches. The only kind of match that he did not referee was The F.A. Cup Final Tie.

On the completion of his twenty-five years service as Secretary of the Lancashire F.A., Mr. Gregson was in 1907 presented with a purse of gold, a silver-mounted pipe, and a silver match box, and his wife was also presented with a gold bracelet.

Mr. Gregson was by profession a photographer at Blackburn, and in his later years at Lytham, and he was in fact for many years the official photographer to The F.A. When X-Rays were first introduced for surgical work, Mr. Gregson took up this important branch of work, and visited many hospitals in the North of England. It will also be seen that Mr. Gregson was also a pioneer in a service that has done wonders in aiding medical work. Mr. Gregson was a skilled ambulance worker, and as such he was said to " have done the work of a dozen men " on that black day of football, when the Grand Stand gave way at Ibrox Park in 1902, when the International Match, Scotland v. England, was in progress. Twenty-five persons were killed, and hundreds injured, the players dressing rooms being used as surgeries, and it was said that the rooms resembled slaughter houses. Mr. Gregson made splints out of floor boards, doors and frame work, and laboured for many hours, and there is no doubt his heroic work in alleviating the sufferings of the injured, enshrined his name in Scottish football history. In the records of that terrible disaster, all name Mr. Gregson as one of those who rendered great service on this sad occasion.

Mr. Gregson was devoted to fishing, and also proficient at Billiards, he was also an ardent smoker. On one occasion when he was rather unwell, he was advised by that typical Lancashire character, " Dick " Birtwistle, to " smoke less and start drinking," this being a dig at Mr. Gregson's abstinence.

During 1909 to 1911 Mr. Gregson had been further experimenting in colour photography, a study of which he had made for over twenty years, and having achieved his object he retired from all his football work, and went to live at Stavely, where he remained until his death, which took place on the 17th April, 1918.

## W. A. DUCKWORTH.

Mr. Duckworth was a stalwart of Bury Football Club, and was ever anxious to keep the flag proudly flying at Gigg Lane. Football he loved as his life. It was to him a passion, which was shared by his wife, his sons, and his daughters. In his early days he played a little cricket, and was a wicket keeper with a useful pair of hands; later in life Mr. Duckworth often had his holidays when Lancashire were playing cricket in the South.

Mr. Duckworth was a thorough Lancashire man, and the architect of his own fortune. He had no affectations, but was very genuine and thorough, and not only formed his own conclusions but adhered to them. For ten years he was President of the Manchester County F.A., and he was first elected a Member of Lancashire Association in 1892, which position he held until his death in 1918.

Mr. Duckworth received his Long Service Medal in 1913, and whilst he will always be remembered for his great work on behalf of Bury Football Club, yet, his cheerfulness and kindness were such that he will be remembered with pleasure by everyone with whom he came in contact.

Mr. Duckworth was also a member of The F.A. Council.

## J. J. HAWORTH.

John James Haworth died in March, 1909, and his passing was a distinct break with the past.

Mr. Haworth was one of the pioneers of Football, a stalwart of Turton F.C., and for many years a most service-able Member on the Council of The L.F.A., to which he was first elected in 1901. For thirty-two years he was the friend, supporter, and adviser of Turton F.C., indeed he was often described as the father of junior football in Bolton and district.

Mr. Haworth died in office in connection with the sport he so admired, but his interests were many. He was a Sidesman at St. Anne' Church, Turton, a Freemason, Oddfellow, and Forrester, and connected with the Bolton Amateur League and the Bolton Wednesday League. He was one of nature's gentlemen, and lived a life of public usefulness, he was Chairman of the League's Sanction Committee, and drafted the Model Rules for the use of Leagues. Mr. Haworth was most systematic in all his work, and he was equally thorough in all he attempted.

Mr. Haworth was not spared to see the fruition of his labours, but the improvements he brought about are a standing memorial to his faithful service.

## MANCHESTER CITY F.C.
### WINNERS OF THE F.A. CUP, 1903-04.

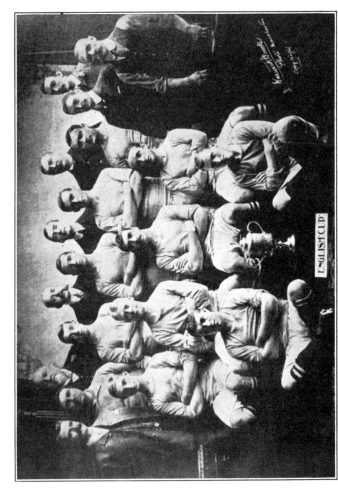

J. Parlby, C. H. Waterhouse, E. Hulton (Chairman), J. E. Chapman, J. Madders.
T. E. Maley (Secretary Manager), J. Hillman, G. Livingstone, J. McMahon, T. Hynds, W. Gillespie, L. W. Furniss,
F. Booth, S. Frost, W. Meredith (Captain). S. B. Ashworth       J. Broad (Trainer),

# CHAPTER XXV.

## THE ORIGIN AND RISE OF THE CENTRAL LEAGUE.

### By J. E. Mangnall.

*The origin and rise of the Central League. Formed 1911. The Founders and First Members. League's Rise and Progress. Present Officials.*

About half way through the month of May, 1911, the League clubs had reason to complain of the attitude adopted by the other clubs, and particularly those in the Second Division, Lancashire Combination. In the past the League clubs had loyally obeyed the rules, although they had been out-voted as the result of sectional meetings held for the purpose, and on one occasion an adjourned Annual Meeting was necessary. Prior to the Annual Meeting—May, 1911, a caucus meeting of sixteen clubs was held. I do not pretend to a knowledge of what transpired at that meeting, but it was suggested that the club calling the meeting was anxious to have one of its members on the Management Committee; that members of League clubs should be opposed, particularly those from Bolton. However, that may be, it is significant that Messrs. J. J. Bentley, T. Y. Ritson, and J. T. Howcroft, were thrown off the Committee.

The League Clubs were indignant and determined not to tolerate these caucus meetings any longer. As Secretary of the Club I knew that Manchester United had not only made up its mind to withdraw from the Lancashire Combination, but that its intention was to make application for admission to one of the Manchester Leagues. I then submitted a scheme to Mr. J. H. Davies, President, and he gave me authority to proceed carte blanche as best I thought. Of the clubs interviewed, I got promises of support from Bolton Wanderers, Bury, Crewe Alexandra, Glossop, Manchester City, Manchester United, Oldham Athletic, Preston North End, Stockport County, and Southport Central.

M

The idea at that time—if no more clubs linked up—was
to fill in the vacant Saturdays by means of a subsidiary
competition.    After an Annual General Meeting of the
L.F.A. at the Winter Gardens, Blackpool, on May 24th,
1911, I called a private meeting.  The following clubs were
represented : Blackpool, Blackburn Rovers, Bolton Wanderers, Burnley, Bury, Everton, Liverpool, Manchester
City, Manchester United, Oldham Athletic, and Preston
North End.  Mr. W. A. Wilkinson (Manchester City), was
invited to take the Chair, Mr. W. C. Cuff (Everton), was
requested to act as Honorary Secretary, pro. tem.    The
Chairman remarked that the members present were invited
together to discuss the treatment meted out to them by the
non-League Clubs of the Lancashire Combination, and referred to the unsettled feeling that had existed during the
past few Seasons, and to the unsportsmanlike action in re-
jecting three valued members of the Management Committee.

The members present strongly condemned the recent
actions of the non-League clubs, and expressed their willingness to withdraw from Membership of the Lancashire
Combination, although several were unable to pledge their
clubs until they had discussed and considered the position.

The meeting therefore stood adjourned to May 28th,
1911, in London, at which meeting all the Lancashire clubs
in the League, in addition to Stockport County and Glossop,
were represented.

The Chairman (Mr. W. A. Wilkinson), gave a resume
of the proceedings at Blackpool, and it was resolved '' that
Messrs. Knowles (Darwen), Rigg (Rochdale), and Fletcher
(Chester), be admitted to the meeting.''  Each gentleman
addressed the meeting and urged the members to
reconsider their position, and continue to work with the
non-League clubs in the Lancashire Combination, at any
rate for another Season.    The deputation were thanked
and withdrew.

It was resolved '' That the League clubs, Members of
the Lancashire Combination, resign from that Combination,
and form a new League, and that application be made to

The F.A. for affiliation, and that a meeting of the members be held at Manchester on a date to be fixed by a Sub-Committee to consider name, rules, etc." The following were appointed a Sub-Committee : Messrs. Wilkinson, Barcroft, Clayton, Houghton, Mangnall, and the Secretary.

At a meeting of the Sub-Committee held at the Imperial Hotel, London, on May 29th, 1911, it was Resolved : " That the new League be called the Central League." The Chairman and Secretary were deputed to prepare a set of rules. The Secretary reported that the thirteen League clubs had resigned their membership of the Lancashire Combination. A meeting of clubs was held at the Mosley Hotel, Manchester, on June 13th, 1911, Mr. W. A. Wilkinson presiding. The roll was signed by the representatives of the thirteen clubs.

It was unanimously resolved that the League consist of eighteen clubs.

A representative from each applying club, except Barnsley, attended and spoke in support of its application. The poll resulted as follows :—

| | |
|---|---|
| Southport Central | 13 votes. |
| Huddersfield | 12 votes. |
| Rochdale | 11 votes. |
| Barnsley | 10 votes. |
| Crewe Alexandra | 10 votes. |
| St. Helen's Recs. | 3 votes. |
| Eccles Borough | 2 votes. |
| Wrexham | 2 votes. |
| Macclesfield | 1 vote. |
| Northern Nomads | 1 vote. |
| South Liverpool | 0 votes. |
| Tranmere Rovers | 0 votes. |

The Chairman thereupon declared Southport Central, Huddersfield Town, Rochdale, Barnsley, and Crewe Alexandra, duly elected members of the Central League.

Mr. Wilkinson proposed, Mr. Houghton seconded, and it was unanimously resolved that Mr. J. McKenna be elected President.

Mr. H. S. Hamer (Bury), was appointed Hon·
Treasurer.

Mr. W. C. Cuff (Everton), was appointed Hon. Secretary, pro. tem·

Messrs. T. A. Barcroft, W. R. Clayton, T. Houghton, J.
E. Mangnall, and W. A. Wilkinson, with the President,
Treasurer, and Secretary, were appointed a Committee of
Management

Overtures, on three occasions have been made to extend the League· The last effort was on April 22nd, 1926,
when a scheme was brought forward suggesting that The
Central League should be geographically divided into
Northern and Southern sections, 22 Clubs in each. It was
Resolved : " That in the opinion of the members the time
for extension of the Central League is not opportune."

Of the seventeen Secretaries acting in that capacity
at the formation of The Central League all have re-
linguished that office, except Mr· T. A. Barcroft (Blackpool).

Although they were elected at the formation, Barnsley,
Huddersfield Town, and Rochdale, had to forego the
honour, and play in their original Competition for a further
Season. As Lincoln City and Burslem Port Vale were pro-
mised election to The Central League upon certain terms,
in case two or more clubs were rejected by the League's
Sanction Committee, they were admitted to membership·
Lincoln City won the first Championship, with Burslem
Port Vale runners-up. The League, therefore, in the year
of its inception consisted of seventeen clubs.

The present Officials are :—

President : Mr. J. McKenna.

Hon. Treasurer : Mr. T. A. Barcroft.

Hon. Secretary : Mr· W. C. Cuff.

Management Committee : Messrs. W. I. Bassett, W.
E. Bracewell, Hilton Crowther, H. P. Hardman, J. E.
Mangnall and A. E. Nicholls·

Board of Appeal : Messrs. E. Case, R. E. Lythgoe, and
C. E. Sutcliffe.

Auditors : Messrs. J. Nicholson and Allan Welch·

# CHAPTER XXVI.

## LANCASHIRE'S SENIOR CLUBS.

*This chapter and succeeding ones have reference to the formation, rise, and progress of the seventeen Senior Clubs in the County. It is impossible to give a full history of each Club, but a concise review of each of the Clubs concerned is presented to the readers.*

## ACCRINGTON STANLEY.

Accrington Stanley may be regarded as the successors of Accrington, who were amongst the Clubs which joined the Football League at its formation. The old Club fell on evil times because it could not keep pace with the times, and after five years in the First Division ceased to exist. Sandwiched between Blackburn and Burnley the financial strain was too great, and the Club which had given us the brothers Horne, McLellan, Stevenson, Bob Bryce, Jud-Howarth, Barbour, Wilkinson, Arnold Whittaker, and others, ceased its operations, and after a generation, we come to the doings of a Club which started with little ambition and pretention. You can never kill memories, and when the question of a Third Division of The Football League cropped up, Accrington Stanley set out to present its claim for consideration. The knowledge that Accrington had been crushed out between the two North-East Lancashire First Division Clubs did not discourage them. If Accrington could run a First Division team in 1888 and 1889, why not Accrington Stanley in 1921, thus when the Third Division, Northern Section, was formed, the Stanley Club was included amongst the twenty selected. The first two Seasons saw them maintaining a fairly high standard, then they began to lose ground, until at the end of Season 1926-27 they finished in the bottom two.

## ACCRINGTON STANLEY F.C.
### WINNERS OF JUNIOR CUP, 1920-21.

J. Jacques, E. Chadwick, F. Heyes, G. E. Holman, R. Cragg, C. Smithies, G. Chapman, G. Wilson, J. Yates, J. Tattersall,
H. Smethurst, A. Colwell, T. Heslop, J. Richardson, T. Pendergast, J. Sutcliffe, A. Studdard, E. Hargreaves.
Seated : J. Brown, J. Hollard, J. Miller, C. Pearson, P. Nelis, P. Quigley, A. Stevenson, S. T. Pilkington (Secretary), F.
Brennand, J. Parramore, W. H. Pilkington (Mascot).

At times they have promised better things, and flattered to deceive, and in Season 1925-26 ran into the Final for the Lancashire Cup, being beaten by Bury on the ground of the Bolton Wanderers Club. Stanley have still something to think about, and something to emulate. Their predecessors, Accrington, won the Lancashire Cup in the second year of the Competition, and for two successive Seasons in 1887-88 and 1888-89. Stanley also won the Junior Cup in 1920-21. Fortunately they have an ambitious Directorate under the Chairmanship of Mr. Cunliffe, and with the advice of that old Villa and Bradford City player, Ernest Blackburn, ought yet to make things hum. The ground question has been handled in business like fashion, but it is the team that wins games, and gains promotion. Nelson did the trick in 1922-23, but did not stick it. Stanley will always have serious Lancashire rivals in Nelson and Rochdale, whilst Southport and Wigan Borough may come along any season. It would be a proud day for our friend, Richard Watson, if Stanley won the Northern Section Shield, but the Club must go on building. Patience and perseverance can overcome every difficulty.

Accrington's glories are memories, Stanley's triumphs have yet to come. On, Stanley on !

The original Accrington Club was formed in 1878, the title changed to Accrington Stanley in 1893, and in 1921, it became " Accrington Stanley (1921), Limited)."

## BARROW F.C.

Poor luckless Barrow ! Oh that I could write words of inspiration, and invest the Club with that spirit of faith which conquers all things. Of patience they have a goodly share, hope with them is eternal, and sooner or later many would delight to see them gain the reward of their incessant toil. Out of the world, almost amongst the mountains they stand in a sphere of splendid isolation. Like Wigan

Borough, Rochdale and Halifax Town, they have fought
to get a footing in an old Rugby centre, and through all
their struggles William Dickinson has stood by and often
for the Club, believing that in the end all will be well. Does
luck run in cycles? Surely at Barrow their luck seems always out. In Seasons 1925-26 and 1926-27 the Club finished
at the bottom of the Northern Section. Bad trade has been
their undoing. If only the special trade of Barrow could
be revived so that the people had money to spend on
pleasure, the Barrow Club would be in clover.

The Clubs of The Football League have been very
considerate, and have not sought to punish the Club by
adding to its misfortune. Barrow without the Football
League would be a Club without a shelter, but you cannot go on expecting favours year after year. The wooden
spoon is the most despised trophy in football, and it is a
sure step to rejection. Barrow must mark my words. It
is no use paying the price of a Derby winner for an old war-
horse, nor is it wise to pay First Division wages to players
not good enough for the Second. Above all, Northern
Section football is a business proposition. There are
players who are paid to play, who play for their pay, and
others who think their play deserves more pay. Barrow
must find the aspiring youths who are triers, and cut their
coat according to their cloth. Barrow is the great centre
of the Furness District. Of ambition they have their share,
of expectation not a little, but as yet, and year after year,
they have nothing to show but unfulfilled promises. I
remember Workington, Frizington Athletic, Moss Bay
Exchange, Cleator Moor Athletic, and other Clubs in
other days. Cannot they supply Barrow with a sparkling
team that would win a much better public interest and
support, and give better results on the field of play? Luck
may turn. if not we must turn it. We must not make luck
responsible for our own failures. so Barrow, please buck
up.

There was a Barrow Club formed in 1902, since which
there have been two or three schemes of re-organisation.

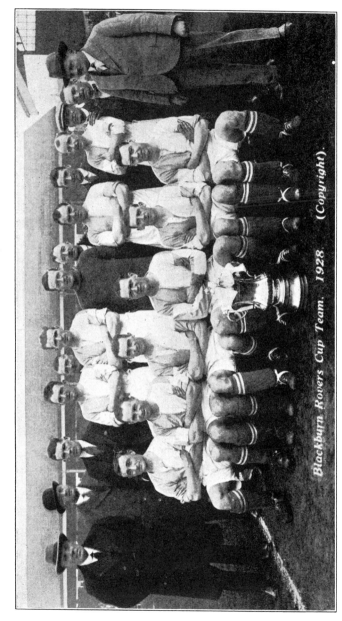

BLACKBURN ROVERS F.C.
WINNERS OF THE F.A. CUP, 1927-28.

*Blackburn Rovers Cup Team. 1928.* (Copyright).

Back Row : J. W. Walsh (Chairman), R. Crompton (Director), T. Mitchell, A. F. Campbell, J. Eddleston (Director), W. Rankin, J. C. Crawford, J. H. Chadburn (Director), J. Hutton, R. Roxburgh, H. Jones, M. Atherton (Trainer), P. B. Holland, A. Barritt (Secretary).

Front Row : G. Thornewell, S. C. Puddefoot, J. Roscamp, H. Healless (Captain), T. McLean, and A. Rigby.

## BLACKBURN  ROVERS  F.C.

To try and give in concise form anything in the nature
of a record of the Rovers Club is impossible, and happily
I am spared the need, for in connection with the Jubilee
of the Club, a full and interesting History was published,
hence to those who have a copy it is only necessary to
add a brief P.S. to bring the History up to date. Those who
did not purchase a copy ought at once to remedy their
oversight. In it is told in most interesting style the story
of the Club's good and ill fortune, from its formation in
1875 to its Jubilee in 1925. Every page is of interest and
full of information which every football enthusiast should
read. The story of each of the five occasions when the
Rovers won the Cup. Thrice in succession, 1883-84, 1884-
85, and 1885-86. the Rovers were Cup winners, beating the
famous Queen's Park on the first two occasions, and West
Bromwich Albion on the last.

The changes in the constitution of a team have always
a prejudicial affect, and for three years the Rovers failed
to reach the Final. but rose in their majesty to win the
Cup in Seasons 1889-90 and 1890-91. Having regard to
the strength of the Clubs entering the contest during the
period of the Rovers' triumphs, the later feats are far
greater than the victory of the Club in the early days of
the Competition. Then came a break in their Cup Tie
history, and to their dismay they had the mortification of
seeing the record number of wins pass to Aston Villa, and
it was not until the Season just ended that the Rovers again
attained a superiority and carried off the Cup. beating
Huddersfield Town at Wembley by 3—1. Their latest
triumph was perhaps their greatest, for Huddersfield Town
had been acclaimed as the wonder team. The knowing
ones, full of daring, asserted that the Cup was a gift for
the Yorkshire team, who were expected not only to win
the Cup, but also the League Championship.

We are indeed grateful to the Rovers for enriching
our Jubilee Year by bringing The F.A. Cup to Lancashire.

I am not going to recall all the famous players who have worn the blue and white shirts. Their glory can never fade, and amongst the portraits on other pages will be found those of many whose names are inseparable from the game. To those must be added the names of the Cup winners last Season. There will be some who will give a special word of praise to various players, yet those who saw the game realised that it was the team as a team that won the game in such masterly fashion. Probably Harry Healless, if asked, might take a risk. I will not, for he of all others, must have been so proud of all the other ten that he would concede that every man was worthy of his colleagues.

Although the Rovers had a quiet Cup Tie period we must not forget that in 1911-12, and again in 1913-14, when no one decried the standard of football, the Rovers won the League Championship, a Competition in which they were never Runners-up. We old stagers like to compare the new with the old. So be it.

I make bold to say that though the Rovers may have had greater individual players they never fielded a better team as a team, than in last Season's Cup Final, a match in which we saw linked the new with the old, for Robert Crompton had his hand in their last triumph, though he could never get hold of a medal for himself. Perhaps the present Directors will appreciate that off the field he wielded a greater influence than on it.

The Rovers have won the Lancashire Cup eleven times, four years in succession, later they won it twice in succession, in three of four Seasons, whilst at a later period they won it three times in five successive Seasons. As a reminder, but with the kindliest of feelings may I remind them that the last occasion was in 1910-11. It seems a long time since, for such famous Cup winners. Another " win " is about due.

The Chairman of the Club is Mr. Will Walsh, and the Secretary-Manager is Mr. A. Barritt, who was previously Assistant to Mr. John Haworth at Turf Moor, Burnley.

## BLACKPOOL F.C.

Founded in 1887 and one of the stalwarts of the old Lancashire League. From its formation full of promise and enthusiasm, but in The Football League always failing us at the last minute. They once shocked Sheffield United by accepting a tempting bait to play an English Cup Tie at Sheffield, though drawn to play at Blackpool, and had the audacity and ability to win. They have had the audacity to tell us over and over again that they were bent on promotion, but have never as yet fulfilled their promise. Why? They have the most enthusiastic Board of any football Club in the Kingdom. Since R. B. Middleton left Blackpool to take charge of Blackburn Rovers, our old friend, Tom Barcroft, has discharged in a Honorary capacity the duties of Secretary. They have had Managers who we were told were going to carry Blackpool into the First Division. They have transferred players who have carried on in First Division teams, and are now amongst the best. Their transferred players have won International and Inter-League honours. They have had on their pay roll, goalkeepers like Hacking, backs like Jones, half-backs like Wilson, and forwards like Gill, Mee, Hardman and Cox. Yet where are they to-day? Parted with an International team, yet rushing hither and thither to make good the gaps.

The town is favoured by all. They have built luxurious stands and found favour for Amateur trial and International games, but as I write, the Club is under the horrid spectre of relegation. I look at the Board, past and present, and recall such pioneers as Ted Little, Fred Seed and Sam Butterworth. Such stalwarts as Albert Hargreaves, financial friends like Sir Lindsay Parkinson, yet the Club flounders. An old Army Officer for his michievous peccadilloes blamed the climate. Is the Blackpool air too strong? Or is life in Blackpool not conducive to success? I must not forget that players of other Clubs have resided at Blackpool.

**BLACKPOOL F.C.**
WINNERS OF JUNIOR CUP, 1890-91.

W. B. Corry, J. Cardwell, L. Wright, H. Parr, S. Whittaker.
A. Bond, H. Tyrer, J. Pittaway, J. Cookson, J. Atkinson.
H. Woods, H. Sturzaker, L. Parr.

Blackpool have never won The F.A. Cup or the Lancashire Cup. In seasons 1887-88 and 1890-91 they won the Lancashire Junior Cup, and in 1913-14 reached the Final of the Lancashire Cup, to be beaten by Manchester United, and again in 1924-25 to be beaten by Bolton Wanderers. It might appear that a change of ground would do them good, but they must fight shy of Bolton where they lost both Lancashire Cup Finals.

The Club's first officials were, Alderman John Bickerstaff. President, Joe Hill, Treasurer, John Anderton, Secretary. The first Directors were Messrs. W. Bond, E. Little, L. Seed, R. Swarbrick, J. Walmsley, with T. Sefton, as Secretary.

The present Chairman is Mr. Sam Butterworth, Mr. Albert Hargreaves is the Vice-Chairman, and Mr. T. A. Barcroft. the smiling and indefatigable Hon. Secretary.

# CHAPTER XXVII.

## LANCASHIRE'S SENIOR CLUBS—*continued.*

### BOLTON WANDERERS

What a name, what a Club, and what a team ! Yet I ask is the Wanderers' Club any stronger in playing strength than in the days of Powell, Roberts, Vaughan, Brogan and Davenport ? Is their defence any better than the immortal trio Sutcliffe, Somerville and Jones ? Wherein then lies the success of the post war team compared with the teams in the 80's and 90's and early in the present century ? Has it been in Management ? Nay, surely such men as J. J. Bentley, Peter Ward, and Will Settle, only to mention three, knew as much about football and footballers as any man living to-day. Then their late President, Mr. J. H. Makent, was with the Club for near on half a century. Like many more Lancashire clubs, it has had its dark days and trying ordeals, and in the fight for existence, and in paving the way to fortune, there were three bosom chums in John Bentley, Walter Taylor, and Tom Gregson, who saved the Club from irretrievable ruin. Later our old friend, Harry Downs, who knows perhaps more of Lancashire football in all its grades and phases than any living man, took over the reins of office as Secretary in succession to Mr. Bentley. The team no matter who was introduced could never do better in a playing sense than win the Lancashire Cup. In the F.A. Cup Competition semi-final stages they seemed fated to run up against Notts County, and only once pre-war did they reach the Final, and then to be beaten by Manchester City by a goal, which though City assert was a good one, Mr. Tom Ritson has, however, thousands of supporters who believe and argue otherwise. Since the war the Wanderers have proved particularly strong in The F.A. Cup Competition,

**BOLTON WANDERERS F.C.**

WINNERS OF THE F.A. CUP, 1922-23.    FIRST FINAL AT WEMBLEY.

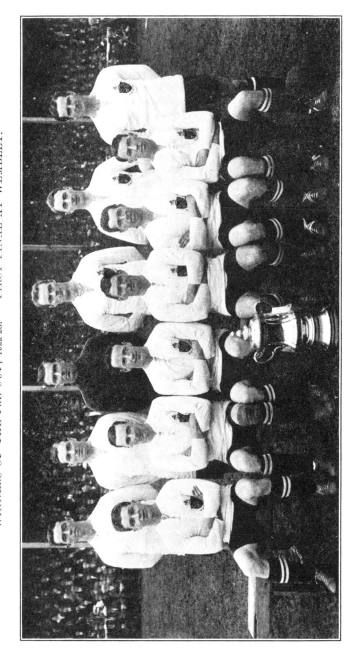

Back row (left to right) : H. Nuttall, R. Haworth, R. H. Pym, J. Seddon, W. Jennings, W. J. Rowley.
Front Row (left to right) : W. Butler, D. B. N. Jack, J. R. Smith, J. Smith (Captain), E. T. Vizard, A. Finney.

and took part in the first memorable Final at Wembley, when in consequence of an incomplete ground and the population equal to a huge town desiring to see the game, 90,520 persons paid at the turnstiles, and 35,527 ticket holders were admitted, giving a total of 126,047. Thousands got in free, and thousands never got in at all. The "gate" amounted to £27,776, and the Wanderers Club received £8,070 16s. 11d. from the Semi-Final and Final. Just imagine it, and compare it with Burnley running a whole season with receipts less than £2,000. In the change from struggle to affluence, there has been a gradual paving of the way, and the march of progress during the 50 years of the Club's history, seems like a chapter from some book of fiction.

At its commencement the Club was a Sunday School Club known as Christ Church, and actually had its existence under that name in 1874. The name of the Club was not changed and the present name adopted until 1877, so that the Club reached its jubilee as Bolton Wanderers last year. Although the Club in its early stages had two or three rough and ready pitches, the Club has practically only known two grounds, Pike's Lane and Burnden Park.

If we recall the names of the great players of the past who have worn the Wanderers Colours, such as Struthers, Steele, Sutcliffe, Powell, Roberts, Brogan, Davenport, Somerville, Jones and a host of others, we should merely recall names of whom Pym, Finney, Seddon, Butler, Jack, Nuttall, Joe Smith, and Vizard are worthy successors.

Bolton Wanderers was one of the moving spirits in the fight for the legalisation of professionalism, and even yet they chuckle over the way they fooled a delegation of The Football Association by palming off as the original books of the Club, a duplicate set carefully written up by the Secretary for the purpose, and upon the accuracy and excellent manner in which the books were kept he was complimented by the Commission. But you cannot carry on a deception for ever, and Bolton Wanderers came out into

N

the open and joined the British Association. During the fight for recognition, none rendered greater assistance than Mr. Peter Parkinson at one time President of the Club.

Mr. J. J. Bentley became Secretary in February, 1885, in succession to Mr. Tom Rawsthorne, and his influence on the Club was such that during the remainder of the season the team played 28 matches, winning 25 and drawing 3.

The Wanderers ground at Burnden Park was opened on 17th August, 1895, with a visit by Preston North End. Prior thereto, the Club had some difficulty in finding shareholders who had to be tempted to take up 25 shares by the offer of a medal entitling the holder to two season tickets in perpetuity. We have not the space to follow the Club through its existence at Burnden Park, the ground has been gradually improved, the Club's financial position made as safe as the Bank of England, and Mr. W. Hamer and his colleagues have had a very happy time for some years, due to wise management and the capability of Mr. C. E. Foweraker. To-day the Club owns the ground and the vacant land adjoining, and some day we or our successors will see the ground at Burnden Park equipped with the latest type of grand stand and with ample covered accommodation to meet the requirements of the most attractive games.

The Lancashire Football Association have much reason to be grateful to its Clubs for their loyalty, and none have been more considerate and helpful than the Bolton Wanderers F.C.

As we go to press, arrangements have been made for our Jubilee Match, Lancashire v. a Team selected by The F.A., to be played at Burnden Park on 10th October, 1928.

BURNLEY.

If ever a Club was called on to start at the bottom, it was the Burnley Football Club. Prior to season 1881-82 Rugby was the only style of game played in the town, and when the change over to Association was decided on, the

**BURNLEY F.C.**

WINNERS OF THE F.A. CUP, 1913-14.

E. Edwards (Trainer), T. Bamford, R. W. Sewell, D. Taylor.
W. Nesbitt, R. Lindley, B. C. Freeman, E. Hodgson, E. Mosscrop.
G. Halley, T. W. Boyle (Captain), W. Watson.

**BURY F.C.**

WINNERS OF THE F.A. CUP, 1902-03.

J. Johnson, J. Lindsay, F. Thorpe, H. Montieth, G. W. Ross (Captain), J. McEwan.
W. Richards, W. Wood, C. Sagar, J. Leeming, J. Plant.

players had to try and learn the new game. They knew that success only awaited on perseverance, and that defeat or failure whilst learning must never discourage. In those days there was no call for goal scoring to be made easier, for as an old player says " Goals were so easily scored against us that we are thankful records were not kept in those days." The players needed tutors, and found help and advice from players borrowed from Accrington, Darwen, and Clitheroe. The Burnley Club had much to thank their neighbours from Accrington for first tutoring them in the arts of football, and also turning their attention to making serious efforts to build up a great team. Old Burnley people will readily recall Tom Bryce (the brother of Bob of Accrington fame), Harper, Gair, Friel, Arthur, Marshall, Macrae, Shiel, Beattie, and McNee, of the early professional days who gradually ousted such locals as Wigglesworth, Sam Hargreaves, Leonard Metcalf, Tom Cross, Charlie Fulton, Arthur Birley, Harry Walton, and Tom Midgley, just as they had taken the place of much earlier stagers as Harry Bradshaw, Fergie Slater, J. W. Holden, C. E. Sutcliffe W. Brown, and others.

In fact, before we reached the mid-eighties Burnley had secured a Scottish XI., and naturally their players were outlawed by Scotland and came under the ban of The Football Association. You can't keep charging expenses to ground, and paying wages sub-rosa, but what the truth will out; and so Burnley was amongst the Clubs that joined the British Association, and helped to bring about professionalism.

Burnley with Bolton Wanderers were the first professional Clubs to play before Royalty, and aptly, Burnley continued to progress, until they were the first to play before and receive The Football Association Cup from His Majesty the King. Between the two occasions 1886 and 1914, Burnley had built up some splendid teams. Who is there of the old school that will ever forget goalkeepers like Kay and Hillman, backs like Bury, Lang, and McClintock, halves like Jock Abram, W. McFetteridge, and Jack

Keenan, or forwards like Gallocher, McLardie, Lambie, Stewart and Hill, and later Edgar Chadwick. We talk of centre-forwards. Had Burnley ever the equal of Claude Lambie? Oh yes, say a later generation, what of Bert Freeman? Just so, hence I recall such players as Jerry Dawson, David Taylor, Alex Leake, Halley, Boyle and Watson, Kelly, Hodgson, and Mosscrop, and even at the present day Waterfield, Hill, Steel, Cross and Page. Yes Burnley have found the players and filled the bill.

The Club won the Cup in 1914, and The Football League Championship in season 1920-21. For other honours see other pages. Who made the Club? Harry Bradshaw. Sam Thomas. Tom Midgeley, Tom Heaton, Walter Curl. A. F. and C. E. Sutcliffe, George Waddington. Who kept it going? Alderman Edwin Whitehead, Dick Wadge, Robert Thornton. Will Crook. and a few others. Who rebuilt it with the necessary ground alterations and splendid stand accommodation? Harry Windle, W .E. Bracewell, Johnny Catlow, Jimmy Harrison. and a few others. Ne'er may their glory fade.

The Club's present Chairman is Mr. Harry Windle, and the Manager is Mr. A. Pickles. assisted by Mr. Edgar England.

May they see the Club grow in strength and triumphs attained.


## BURY F.C

Formed in 1885. the inception taking place at the Waggon and Horses' Hotel, Bury, followed by a further meeting at the White Horse Hotel, Fleet Street. The Club being a development of the Bury Unitarians and Bury Wesleyans Clubs.

Bury ! The Club that fought against the giants until it had accomplished what seemed almost impossible in rising from comparative obscurity to fame, and making history during the progress. Formed on the 24th April, 1885, the Club played its first game at Little Lever on 5th September of that year, followed a week after by a game at home against Wigan (the Club's home was then at Gigg Lane), and the " gate " amounted to £1 16s. 7d., and at the end of the season there was an adverse balance of £8 0s. 1d., and in addition, outstanding accounts amounting to £68 and no assets.

Every Club that is famous in football to-day has had to start at the bottom, and it is those who faced misfortune and difficulties in the true spirit of progress that have succeeded. Bury has always had friends that would never let the Club go down, and finding players of ability in the town or villages around, soon began to build up a team. George Ross, one of Bury's own products, though born in Scotland, was an International in play, but barred by circumstances of birth and regulations, yet George Ross was paid first 3/-, later increased to 4/- per week, for his services to the Club.

Increasing in strength the Club increased in debt. Is it any wonder when the lavish sum of £50 11s. 8d. was paid for the first covered stand ? The Club became am-bitious, and from the time of the late Mr. H. S. Hamer taking over the work of Secretary, there was for many years marked progress. The advent of players like Steel, who migrated from Bolton Wanderers. and Bob Conway, who was prior thereto with Accrington, fired the ambition of the Bury people, introducing attractive Clubs as visitors, but the team was beaten in the Fourth Round of the Lan-cashire Junior Cup by Blackpool.

The next step was the formation of the Lancashire League which organisation Bury helped to found, and joined in the Competition in its first season 1889-90, running second and winning the Lancashire Junior Cup. About this time Jack Plant joined the Club. and the history for some years was one of continual progress. winning the Lancashire Football Association Cup in 1891-92 at the first time of asking. The total weekly wage of the 11 players was £12. Bury like many other Clubs turned their eyes to Scotland. and the late Mr. W. A. Duckworth had many interesting stories to tell of his poaching days.

The Club made many good bargains both in obtaining players and on the business side of the Club's affairs, but Rossendale people are never tired of telling the story how in season 1892-93 Bury paid the Rossendale Club £80 to change the venue of their F.A. Cup Tie. This cute business transaction became a sad mixture of comedy and tragedy, for Rossendale went to Gigg Lane and won by 7—1.

During their five years connection with the Lancashire Football League the Club finished Champions twice, runners-up twice, and third once. Is it any wonder that the Club aspired to a better Competition, and was admitted to the Second Division of The Football League for season 1894-95, and won the Second Division Shield at their first attempt. Amongst their players at that time were Montgomery, Davidson, Clegg, Ross, Wyllie, Barbour, and Plant, and the wage bill £29 per week. The late Albert Duckworth and Alderman Fred Bradley were the two best known Directors, whilst the late H. S. Hamer was Secretary. In 1894-95 the team gained promotion to the First Division. They found a vast difference between First and Second Division football, and though they maintained membership with the First Division they had to thank the Clubs for an extension of the League at the end of season 1904-05. They finished in the bottom two with Notts County, but the League was increased to 20 Clubs in each Division, and Bury and Notts County called back to their Garden of Eden.

Probably few Clubs with the same limited resources could have equalled Bury's record. The population of the town was the least of all the towns represented in the First Division, hence the Club had to attain and maintain its position by wise and economical management, and when we recall amongst their playing staff, Jimmy Settle, Joe Leeming, Charlie Sagar, Billy Richards. Hibbert and

Wood, along with Jack Plant, we see something of the playing strength of the team in those and subsequent days. Were those players playing to-day what would their value be to the Club? I am not minimising the worth of Fred Heap, Porter, Bradshaw, Bullock, Ball and Amos, but is there a man in or out of Bury who will say that Settle, Sagar, Leeming, Hibbert and Plant, were one whit inferior to any player that played either for Bury or any other Club. Four of them helped to win The F.A. Cup in 1900. Three years later Bury performed the same feat with this remarkable difference that not a goal was scored against the team in the Competition, and 8 of the 11 players had been nursed and developed from juniors at Gigg Lane.

The Club has had its ups and downs. At the end of season 1911-12, the Club was relegated to the Second Division of The Football League, but fought back and won through at the end of season 1923-24. The Club has always had an enthusiastic Directorate. and the Management throughout sound and efficient. and it is no reflection on any other Club, to say that its sequence of Secretaries has never been excelled for ability and reliability. The late Harry Hamer was one of the men that helped to make the Lancashire Football Combination, an organisation in its day perfect in its work. Frank Hamer was a faithful assistant and a typical financier, for he kept the finances of the Club within such bounds of economy that the way was paved to the present financial stability, whilst Arthur Paine is in all his work a perfect model. With enthusiasts like Messrs. H. Duckworth, H. Unsworth, E. Brown, R. Robinson, M. Hamer, and F. Hopkinson, to every one of whom the Bury Football Cub is a real hobby, the success of the Club is assured.

The Chairman of the Club is Mr. Herbert Duckworth (a worthy son of a worthy Sire. Albert Duckworth), the Club Secretary is Arthur Paine, formerly of Lancaster Town. and the Manager is our old friend, Percy Smith, one time player of Preston North End and Blackburn Rovers, and who prior to his appointment at Bury, was in charge of the Nelson Club.

## EVERTON F.C.

CHAMPIONS OF THE FOOTBALL LEAGUE. DIVISION I. 1927-28.

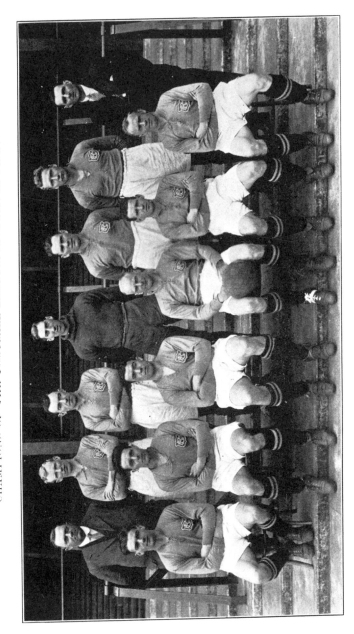

Standing: T. H. McIntosh (Sec.-Manager), J. Kelly, H. Hart, A. L. Davies, J. O'Donnell, A. E. Virr, H. E. Cooke (Trainer).
Seated: E. Critchley, G. S. Martin, W. R. Dean, W. Cresswell, A. Weldon, A. Troup.                [Photo by R. Brown, Liverpool.]

# CHAPTER XXVIII.

## LANCASHIRE SENIOR CLUBS—*continued*.

## EVERTON F.C.

Hail the Champions of The Football League First Division, 1927-28.

The name of the Everton F.C. stands for all that is grand and majestic in the world of football. Happy to-day in having as its Chairman of Directors, Mr. W. C. Cuff, who has had a close association with it from it conception, we can understand the panoramic rise of the Club from the days when as St. Domingo Football Club, it was merely a playing institution of the youths connected with St. Domingo Congregational Church.

Everton's first match was played on 23rd December, 1879 ;they first played at Anfield. but removed to Goodison Park in 1892.

Since joining the Lancashire F.A. in season 1880-81, and rejoicing in a gate of 13/- in 1882. the Club rose almost meteor like, until its honours are now almost beyond number. Let us look at them

Winners of The F.A. Cup in 1905-06. Runners-up in 1892-93. 1896-97 and 1906-07.

They have been 8 times in the Semi-Final.

League Champions 1890-91, 1914-15, and 1927-28. Runners-up 1889-90, 1894-95, 1901-02, 1904-05, 1908-09, 1911-12.

Winners of Lancashire Cup 1896-97 and 1909-10.

To attempt to traverse the history of the Club through all its successes would take far too much space. They have been supplying International players from 1890 down to the present time. and they have never been deposed from the First Division of The Football League, and what is more, during all their association with The Football League, the name of the Club has been associated with play of the highest standard. 'Tis true in seaon 1926-27 the Club was for long in grave danger, but the great cause was injuries to players before the season started. To write of the players from Johnny Holt to W. R. Dean would be one monotonous sequence of eulogies of merit.

The Club has always been enterprising, and in consequence well supported. After a period at Anfield friction arose, a split of which we need only say it gave us two great Clubs instead of one, and the transference of Everton to Goodison Park, the Everton Club has been so strongly supported financially, that the Club is rich in this world's goods, and a ground second to none in the United Kingdom. So rich are they that money is no object, and a team worthy of the Club will always be fielded at Goodison Park, because the Directors readily spot and remedy any weakness on the playing field. Since Dick Molyneux was Secretary until the present time there have been few changes in Management, though the Board has at times been divided into two factions, and for one reason or another football stalwarts like Dr. Whitford and Mr. W. R. Clayton have been lost to the Club. Every Director of the Club has stood high in the esteem of the Citizens of Liverpool, and no matter what factions have been at work, a competent Board has always been left in harness. With Mr. Cuff accustomed to Secretarial duties with the Club, Secretary of the Central League, and a member of the Management Committee of The Football League, in the Chair, the Directorate will never allow the Club to fall from a very high position. Death has removed old figures from the Club of whom there was no one more typical of the phrase " nature's gentleman " than the late Dr. Baxter. His son has succeeded him on the Board.

The present Secretary-Manager is Mr. Tom McIntosh, smiling and genial, especially so when " Dixie " finds the net.

## LIVERPOOL F.C.

The late Tom Watson used to say " My life is full of trouble, we are always either fighting for Championhships, Cups or promotion, or else we are fighting to escape relegation, and every time it is a desperate struggle." The Club started with trouble when Everton went to Goodison. My old friend, Mr. John McKenna could tell the story, for it fought for its ground, its name, its financial strength and every honour the Club has won. The team soon became known as the team of Macs, and the Macs soon made the Club one of the best known in football. Liverpool played its first game under the name of the City on the 1st September, 1892, and for the purpose of paving the way and proving its merit, joined the Lancashire League winning the Championship over Blackpool on goal average. They won the Lancashire League Cup, but some thieves came in the night and stole it away. 'Twas a lesson. Liverpool have won other Cups since, but taken better care of them. After one season in the Lancashire League they were elected to the Second Division of The Football League and won promotion at the first attempt. One season was enough, and losing in the test match to Bury they spent 1895-96 in the Second Division. Again they won promotion and remained in the First Division until the end of season 1903-04, when they found themselves relegated to the Second Division, and again they won back at the first attempt in season 1904-05. Meanwhile they had won the League Championship in 1900-01. Created a record by winning the Second and First Division Championships in successive seasons, viz., 1904-05 and 1905-06, and then reached the climax of their success by winning the First Division Championship in two successive seasons, 1921-22, and 1922-23. They have never won The F.A. Cup, but appeared in the Final in 1914 at Crystal Palace when Burnley won. Four times they have reached the Semi-Finals, and it can only need perseverance to eventually win the coveted honour.

HIS MAJESTY KING GEORGE V. AT HYDE ROAD, MANCHESTER.
MANCHESTER CITY v. LIVERPOOL, PLAYED ON MARCH 27th, 1920.

Let us also record the fact that the season that Liverpool first played in the Second Division of The Football League they played 28 games winning 22, drawing 6, and losing none. The foundation of the Club's success was laid by the late Mr. John Houlding, the late Mr. Edwin Berry, the Chairman, and Messrs. John McKenna, W. E. Barclay and J. J. Ramsey. We talk of transfer fees at the present time, but over 30 years ago " Tityrus " in his "Rise of the Leaguers " tells of efforts made by the present President of The Football League to induce players to come from Scotland to Liverpool and says, " it seemed to require the wealth of Crœsus and a Liverpool shipyard thrown in to tempt them South."

The Liverpool F.C. has included many great players in their ranks from Scott, the greatest Irish International that ever kept goal, to Harry Chambers who has recently been transferred to West Bromwich Albion. The Board has always comprised men of the highest sportmanship. I can never hope to see better sportsmanship than when they failed to win The F.A. Cup at the Crystal Palace, and since that date I have often heard Burnley people express the hope that Liverpool would soon have the good fortune to be winners. It is easy for winners to make friends, but when losers make friends it is a great triumph.

## MANCHESTER CITY F.C.

The Club was formed in 1880, being then known as West Gorton, the father of the Club being W. Chew.

A Club with a history typical of Football. What's in a name? Everything. What success did you find associated with Small Heath, Newton Heath, Leicester Fosse, and Woolwich Arsenal, until they changed their names. So with West Gorton, later its name was changed to Gorton and then to Ardwick. So with Ardwick. Had the Club continued under any of its parochial names which suggested limitation of sphere and ambition, success would have been wanting. It may be surprising, but it is true, that the public like an imposing

# MANCHESTER CITY F.C.

WINNERS OF THE LANCASHIRE CUP, 1927-28, AND ALSO
CHAMPIONS OF THE FOOTBALL LEAGUE,
SECOND DIVISION.

J. G. Ridley,x  S. Gibbons,  S. Cowan,x  P. McCloy,x  M. W. Barrass.x
S Sharp,  T. Tait,x  A. Gray,  L. F. Barber,x  S. W. Austin,x  G. W. Hicks.
A. Horne,  R. S. Marshall,x  J. McMullan,x  T. C. F. Johnson,x  E. F. Brook.x

The players marked (x) appeared in The Lancashire Cup Final Tie v. Bury.

name, and so after Ardwick became Manchester City, in-
significance gave way to importance. Could Ardwick F.C.
ever have migrated to and built the palatial ground at
Maine Road with its accommodation for 80,000 spectators?
Could the name of Ardwick ever have attracted the team
that won The F.A. Cup in 1904, Hillman; Burgess, Mc
Mahon; S. B. Ashworth, Hynds, Frost; Meredith, Livingstone, Gillespie, Turnbull (A.) and Booth. Could the Club
ever have been runners-up of The Football League 1st
Division, as were Manchester City in 1903-04 and 1920-21,
or Champions of the Second Division as were City in 1898-
99, 1902-03 and 1909-10? Such a thing seems incredible.
Would The F.A. ever have looked at Hyde Road
as a ground for a big game which would attract a huge
crowd? No, you must have enterprise, and though men like
Messrs. John Allison, W. A. Wilkinson and Josh Parlby,
saw serious difficulty they knew that in some form or other,
the Club must throw off its shackles of littleness and aim
high.

The Club was not lacking in enterprise at Hyde Road,
but when you went to the ground you felt you were going
along some subterranean passage to an  enclosure  that
precluded enlargement and kept you under confinement
willy nilly. How gentlemen like Messrs. John Chapman
and Sam Anderson lived under such conditions was a mystery. That Ernest Mangnall could ever let his brains have
full scope baffles me. What a blessing it was that the
seeming misfortune of that disastrous fire led the Directors
to look round Manchester, with the result that the Club
now boasts a ground with the largest holding capacity outside Wembley, and with room for further extension and
addition that could make the holding capacity of Wembley
seem insignificant.

In one way Manchester is still primitive in its accommodation. At neither Old Trafford nor Maine Road can
the ordinary 1/- spectator find covered accommodation.
Our City friends launched out freely, but they and Manchester United must provide covered accommodation for

o

the men who do not aspire to Grand Stands on which you sit, but are prepared to stand the game through, yet desire some protection from the weather.

The flag is proudly flying at Maine Road, for City, after a great and epic struggle, have regained the Paradise of the First Division.

In the Club's early days it had struggles and disappointments, then came its advent into The Football League, Second Division, followed by its promotions to, and relegations from, the First Division.

The tragedy of 1925-26 is still fresh in our minds, how that City in seeking the glamour of the " Cup " again lost its position in the First Division.

The struggle was renewed in Season 1926-27, when City lost promotion on goal average, by the 200th part of a goal. Truly, such misfortunes " were enough to bring a Royal Merchant down; " but not the City. The task of regaining admission to the " elect " or " select," was renewed with zeal, determination, and hope, and on Wednesday evening, 25th April, 1928, by a meritorious victory over Leeds United at Leeds, promotion was well and truly won.

Hail to City F.C., Champions of the Second Division on four occasions. May your next triumph be that of Champions of the First Division.

The Club is happy in having as its Chairman so zealous and courteous a gentleman as Mr. Lawrence Furniss, who was a player of the Club when it was named West Gorton, and later was Secretary of the Club when it was named "Ardwick," and who has been associated with City F.C. practically throughout its existence. Mr. Furniss is equally happy in having around him a devoted Board of Directors, and a team of players who are a credit to the Club.

Mr. W. Wild is an efficient, obliging and smiling Secretary.

Maine Road is a great ground, and great crowds assemble there, and the supporters of the Club look for results in keeping with the grounds surroundings and equipment.

## MANCHESTER UNITED.

Formed in 1878 and known as Newton Heath until 1902, when the name was changed to Manchester United.

The story of Manchester United consists of two chapters distinct yet interwoven, for the Club as we see it to-day is but the superstructure which has arisen from the old Newton Heath Club. For years the Club was nothing more than a very ordinary Second Division Club, and though George and Herbert Dale, in conjunction with their Secretary, Alf Albut, succeeded in finding some good players, whether the chemical fumes so strong'y associated with the District, had a prejudicial effect I cannot say, but players like Harry Stafford, Walter Cartwright, Erentz, Dow, McNaught, Clarkin, Donaldson, Cassidy, Doughty and others, would be great players with any Club to-day, but if nothing else could damn a Club that wretched ground at Newton Heath would prove effective. In places hard as flint, with ashes underneath that had become like iron, and in others thick mud, made the ground an impossible one.

With the advent of the late Mr. J. H. Davies who called to his aid the late Mr. J. J. Bentley, the romance of Manchester United began. Mr. J. E. Mangnall was engaged as Secretary Manager, and from that date the rise of Manchester United, as Newton Heath had then become in name, became gradual but complete. The transfer of the ground to Old Trafford was as astute as it was necessary. Fortune hitherto unknown to the Club smiled upon it, and in a short period the Club won every possible honour. With the removal of Mr. Mangnall to the City Club, the United has not found their path so freely strewn with roses, but they boast of a ground which has produced many records and found favour for Internationals and Semi-Finals and Finals in The F.A. Cup Competition, and no wonder seeing the ground holds 72,000.

## MANCHESTER UNITED F.C.
### WINNERS OF THE F.A. CUP, 1908-9.

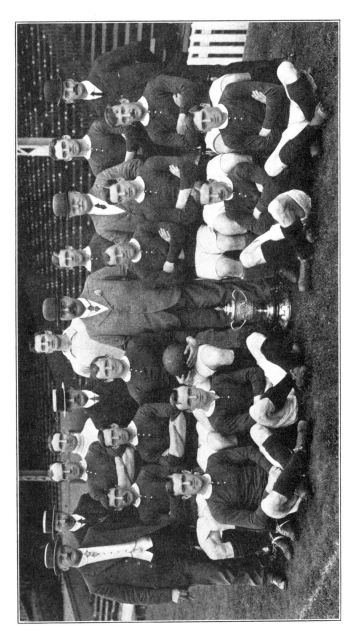

Back Row: J. E. Mangnall (Secretary), F. Bacon (Trainer), J. Picken, H. Edmunds, G. H. Murray (Director), H. Moger, T. Homer, G. H. Lawton (Director), A. Bell, W. R. Deakin (Director).

Middle Row: W. Meredith, R. Duckworth, C. Roberts, J. H. Davies (Director), A. Turnbull, E. West, G. Stacey.

Bottom Row: A. Whalley, L. Hofton, H. Halse, G. Wall.

The F.A. Cup was won in season 1908-09, and the League Championship in 1907-08 and 1910-11, thus it is easily seen that during those four seasons the Club must have had a team worthy to rank with the best, past or present. When we recall backs like Hayes and Stacey, half-backs like Duckworth, Roberts and Bell, and forwards like Meredith, Halse, Turnbull and Wall, we can understand the success of the Club. But players come and go. Father Time puts his hand on them, and the days of youth soon pass, yet the United have maintained a high standard of excellence thanks to such players as Jack Mew, Frank Barson, Clement Hilditch, and Jack Silcock. Under the regime of Managers Robson, Chapman, and Bamlett, the frequenters of Old Trafford have always had the privilege of seeing players of undoubted ability. Spence, Bennion, Jones and Thomas were in the International honours list in 1926-27, and all of them with Silcock in favour last season. The latter perhaps lost a chance through illness.

The Club lost its greatest friend last season in the death of its President, the late Mr. J. H. Davies, but in Messrs. G. H. Lawton, H. P. Hardman, J. Yates, and G. Bedford, the Club have a quartette of enthusiasts to whom football is a natural part of life and its pleasures. In a playing sense probably Harold Hardman has been the Club's greatest adviser, but all four have a distinctive work which is carried through with thoroughness.

## NELSON F.C.

### CHAMPIONS OF THE FOOTBALL LEAGUE. THIRD DIVISION. 1922-23.

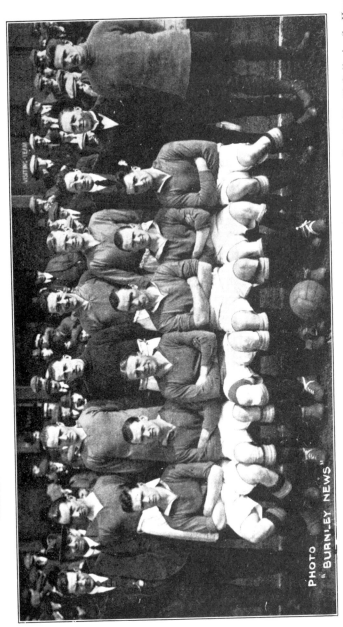

PHOTO
"BURNLEY NEWS"

R. Lilley, W. Hartley (Chairman), F. Steele, C. Rigg, J. Birds, E. Braidwood, J. E. Broadhead, M. McCulloch, S. Hoad.

B. Smith (Trainer).

J. Black, J. Eddleston, A. Wolstenholme, D. Wilson (Player-Manager), R. Crawford, R. Hutchinson.

# CHAPTER XXIX.

## LANCASHIRE'S SENIOR CLUBS—*continued.*

## NELSON.

A name which stands for victory. A Club which typifies continual struggle. Ambition, fight, loss, but continued faith, there you have the short history of the Club. Founded in 1882 the Club struggled about here and there, but until fired by ambition to enter into League warfare, the Club could never find its name written in the annals of note recording success. They joined The Football League when the Northern Section was formed for season 1921-22, gained promotion in season 1922-23, were relegated the following season, and are now fighting for their existence. They have their name to make. They have found and transferred some notable players such as S. J. Wadsworth, now with Huddersneld Town, Hampson, with Blackpool, and Earle, at Burnley. They have tried a measure of enterprise in signing on players like David G. Wilson, and have speculated in Management, but as yet they have not got no where where they could plant their feet firmly.

They have failed for lack of support. The Northern Section has had a rough period through trade depression, and perhaps North-East Lancashire has suffered most. You can't run a big store on a small shopkeepers capital, and you cannot run a football Club long on debts and liabilities. Season 1927-28 has been Nelson's crowning misfortune. I have known Nelson since it was little more than an insignificant village. I have followed the growth of the town through years of ambitious progress. In cricket they glory, in football they have made me ashamed. Season 1922-23 showed that it was possible to gain promotion, but 1923-24 showed that until Nelson would render better support, a higher class of football could not be maintained.

Sometimes we learn more from failure than success, and character is strengthened more by difficulties than ease. Nelson should be amongst Lancashire's best, and I have faith that all will be well. Fortunately, they were re-elected to the Third Division of the Northern Section of The Football League in June last. Application for re-election was an unpleasant experience which must be avoided in future.

## OLDHAM  ATHLETIC.

The rise of Oldham Athletic is almost like a romance. From a little-known Club styled Pine Villa, which had gained some local distinction in the Oldham Junior League, Oldham Athletic sprung. The name was changed, and the new Club started on its romantic career on the 4th July, 1899. Then began the ambition and craving for better football, and to go all out to make new conquests. The Club joined the Manchester Alliance and finished second. In the march of progress the Club joined the Manchester League for four seasons and found a place in the Lancashire Combination in 1904-05. They immediately gained promotion to Division "A." That was the incentive to go all out for election as members of The Football League, but though they appealed to the Clubs at the Annual Meeting they failed to secure election by one vote. At the subsequent Annual Meeting they met the same fate with a reduced vote, and hope vanished.

You never know your luck, and the resignation of Burslem Port Vale provided an unexpected opportunity, and the 'Latics Club was elected by the Management Committee of The Football League to take the place of Burslem Port Vale for season 1907-08. The first season almost brought promotion, for the Club finished third in the table. Season 1909-10 was the 'Latics crowning season. They started badly and the team were voted a lot of

' stiff-uns,'' for the first 5 games, 3 were lost and 2 drawn.
By the end of the year 17 points had been scored for 17
games.    With the New Year came the Club's greatest
fortune, for they gained promotion on goal average, Oldham Athletic, Hull City, and Derby County all finishing
with 53 points.    Manchester City heading the list with 54.

Much of the success of the Club was due first of all to
Alderman Grime and his Directors, and later to the late
Mr. Wm. Heath who succeeded Alderman Grime as Chairman.    Mr. Heath rendered an extended usefulness to the
game by joining the Council of the Lancashire F.A., and
the good work was carried on by Mr. L. P. Stanton and
others, but misfortunes are never to seek.

The 'Latics have from time to time  engaged  many
noted players, but some, such as W. Appleyard and Finlay
Speedie, never settled down to their form, but Alec Downie,
Charlie Roberts, Hugh Moffatt, and a host of others kept
the Club in the forefront, and when we recall such players
as Ted Taylor, David Wilson, and Arthur Dixon, we see
how the name of the Club has been kept in the limelight.
Nor has the merit of the team ever seriously suffered until
the war threw football into the melting pot.    With the
weakening of the defence that severed the old partnership
of Hodson and Cook, eventually the Club at the end of
season 1922-23 dropped into the Second Division.    Alas,
the Second Division had grown in strength, and the fight
to get back is a serious business both from a playing and
financial point of view.    Relegation was the forerunner of
financial troubles, and it is a credit to the directors, management and players, aided by a Supporters' Club that has
rendered valuable financial service, that the Club has been
strengthened in every sense, and last season for a time,
challenged the leaders in the Second Division of The Football League for promotion.

Though the Club parted with such players as Taylor,
Gray, and Matthews, all goalkeepers of International
standard, they have in Hacking a goalkeeper who caught
the eye of the Selectors, and was called on to keep goal

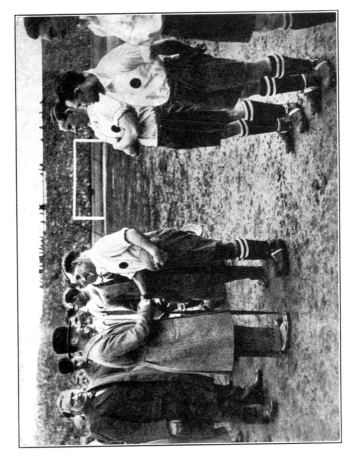

F.A. CUP. FINAL TIE, 1921-22.

HUDDERSFIELD TOWN v. PRESTON NORTH END.

Preston North End Players being introduced to the Duke of York.

for The Football League team v. the Scottish League at Glasgow on 10th March, 1928. The transfer of others like Freeman and Wynne have only proved the ability of the Oldham Athletic management to make good. The Management throughout has been the embodiment of modesty, though at times their modesty has broken out into ambition, yet throughout, the young player discovered in junior football has always found a welcome at Boundary Park.

The 'Latics to-day have other Internationals in the making, but mark my words they will catch them young and bring them on. Could Bob Mellor and his present Directors think of any other policy?

## PRESTON NORTH END.

In the year 1880-81 after a few years of the Rugby Section, a resolution in favour of adopting the Association code was carried. Naturally, the pioneers had to serve their apprenticeship, and receive some sound thrashings ere they were so far masters of the game as to make an equal fight with the best of the Palatine Clubs. After several heavy defeats at the hands of the Rovers, etc., better days came in the year 1883-4.

The local members had improved their play very appreciably, but another factor had an even larger influence, and was indeed the initiation of the policy on which the greatness of the Club was, in large measures, to be built up. The credit of this policy must be awarded to Mr. William Sudell, who took a leading part in securing the field at Deepdale, thoroughly enthusiastic and a splendid judge of football, he took the helm with a strong hand in the early eighties. The coming of certain Scotchmen to Lancashire had not escaped Mr. Sudell's notice, they came ostensibly to obtain work, but in reality to play football. Professionalism was of course illegal. One of the first of

Mr. Sudell's Scotch recruits was none other than the great
Nick Ross, he was captain of the Heart of Midlothian, em-
ployment was obtained for him, and in 1883-84 he was in
North End's team.

This was only the beginning, and soon Georgie
Drummond, Sandy Robertson, D. Russell and J. Gordon
were brought in, and later J. Graham, S. Thomson, J. Ross,
and J. Ferguson, and the excellent local players W. Joy,
F. Dewhurst, R. Howarth, B. Robinson, C. Duckworth,
and W. C. Rose, joined the ranks.

In 1883-84, the first season in which there is a complete
and reliable record of the matches played, it is found that
out of the 44 matches played no less than 30 were won
and only 4 lost, the remainder being drawn, and for the
next ten years there was always a wide margin in North
End's favour on the season's play.

Mr. Sudell was determined to have good players from
Scotland at all costs, and North End's meeting with Upton
Park at Preston in January, 1884, marked a crisis. There
were six Scotchmen in the side. The match was drawn,
whereupon Upton Park protested on the ground that North
End were guilty of paying their players. Mr. Sudell ad-
mitted the charge, and North End was expelled, and in
July of the following year Professionalism was legalised.

It was at this time that North End won the Cup and
League unbeaten, and without a goal being scored against
them in the Cup Competition. Turning to the League,
we find that North End were one of the 5 Clubs to which
Mr. McGregor sent his original letter suggesting a
formation of the League, this in March, 1888. This idea
met with favour, and the following season the League was
in operation with 12 Clubs. The Prestonians led at the
finish by obtaining 40 points out of a possible 44. North
End also fought great battles with the famous Corinthians,
and the Scottish cracks, Queen's Park, and it was in 1886-
87, that Preston broke Scotland's heart by wiping out the
famous old Queen's Park by 6—1, the worst defeat they
had ever experienced in their history.

In time the ranks were weakened and funds required, so in the summer of 1893 a limited liability company was formed.

There is a standard which can be reached but not maintained, and though Preston North End became known as The Old Invincibles, being Finalists for The F.A. Cup in 1887-88 and winning the trophy in 1888-89, the improvement of other clubs and a keener competition had its effect. Although they won The Football League Championship in 1888-89, being undefeated in the Competition, and won it again the following season, records prove that thereafter they had several lean seasons, dropping into the Second Divisin at the end of Season 1900-01. They won promotion 3 years later, but went down at the close of 1911-12, were out of the First Division for one season, then in for a season and out for a season again, but dropped out at the end of 1924-25.

Although North End have had such stars as Peter Mc Bride and Joe McCall in the intervening years, and have spent a fortune in trying to get back, they have not won their way back. Since the war there have been dramatic changes in the personnel of the team, several changes in Management, a Shareholders Committee keeping watch on the doings of the Club, and notable changes in directorate, many old Prestonians sigh tor the days when Will Ord, Tom Houghton, and Walter Pomfret, were guiding the destinies of the Club. Still there are notable figures on the Board, and one cannot conceive that Sir Meyrick Hollins, Jim Taylor, and others, will rest content until Preston North End reaches its old honoured position.

It seems remarkable that the Old Invincibles should have only won The F.A. Cup on one occasion, viz. season 1888-89. They reached the Final in 1887-88 and again in 1921-22, and to this day there are people in Preston who when you refer to the penalty kick by which their opponents won the Cup shake their heads and say, " It was never a penalty kick in this world."

The Club has introduced other great sportsmen to public notice, such as the late Mr. W. E. Ord and the late Mr. Tom Houghton. One of its early Secretaries was Mr. Tom Charnley, now the Secretary of The Football League, who is universally regarded as the most prompt, patient, and painstaking official connected with the game. Of late there have been numerous Secretarial and Managerial changes, all indicative of a keen determination to place the Club in its old honoured position. Sir Meyrick Hollins is not the man to be content with anything but the best, nor are the Directors likely to be weighed down unduly by difficulties. The proud spirit of the town never dies, and the Club is typical of the people.

# CHAPTER XXX.

## LANCASHIRE'S SENIOR CLUBS—continued.

## ROCHDALE F.C.

The History of the Rochdale A.F.C. is one of struggle against difficulties that have only been overcome by the courage and sacrifice of a stout band of enthusiasts for the Association game. Rugby had got a firm foothold in the town long before a soccer club was established, and a club under the name of Rochdale Town had a short and stormy career. This club became defunct owing to financial difficulties, and for a time there was not a Senior Association club in the town

The present club was formed in 1907, and the writer is familiar with the affairs of Rochdale from that time, and he has no hesitation in stating that all those associated with the club have every reason to be proud of their achievements. The first Season saw the club in the Manchester League, and at the close Rochdale stood tenth in the League, having the record, Played 30; Won 10, Lost 12, Drawn 8, Points 28, Goals for 49, against 28. The next Season saw Rochdale transferred to the Second Division of the Lancashire Combination, and singularly they again finished in the tenth position. But the crowds at the matches were small, for the football was not good enough to woo the Rugbyites, and in 1909-10 the Directors cast their bread upon the waters, and a combination of players was secured that was better than any Rochdale had previously seen. It was a successul venture, for in addition to winning promotion to the First Division of the Lancashire Combination, Rochdale won the Lancashire Junior Cup, and they took over a thousand spectators to Bolton to see them win.

In the higher circles Rochdale had a successful time, for they topped the Combination, and made history by beating Stockport County in the fourth qualifying round for the English Cup, but in the next round were dismissed by Luton after a drawn game at Rochdale.

The Season 1912-13 saw Rochdale Members of the Central League, and they had a successful time. Each year they made application for a place in the Second Division of The Football League, but without success. The War saw Rochdale amongst the premier clubs, and so good was their record that it was a great disappointment when they were refused a position in the Second Division in the Season 1919-20.

The idea of a Third Division emanated from Rochdale, and since it was formed, Rochdale have made big efforts to earn promotion, but on three occasions have failed by a very narrow margin. There is a soccer public in Rochdale, and Second Division football will pay. To get there is the problem, for the management have always been short of capital.

Rochdale have provided some good players for various Senior Clubs, and one always remembered is Tommy Fleetwood, who played so long and successfully for Everton. Then Mort. who went to Aston Villa, Bissett to Middlesbrough, Prouse to Fulham, and there are many others.

Rochdale are hoping that after twenty-one struggling years the 22nd will see them realise their ambition—a team in the Second Division.

Mr. J. G. Peart is the Club Secretary, and he lives in hope of triumphs yet to come.

## SOUTHPORT F.C.

Southport, formerly known as Southport Central, then as Southport Vulcan, and now as Southport, at one time content to be regarded as a homely seaside Club, with little greater pretentions in the days of our old friend, T. G. Shipley's Secretaryship as the Club that lived to provide holiday fare for visitors to Southport, and cared nothing about the rest of their matches, have now some pretention to win fame and gain promotion to the Second Division of The Football League.  As to their past we need trouble little, for only on rare occasions have they carved their name on the annals of fame.  That spirit of lethargy has been in spite of the ambitious desires of Mr. E. Clayton, J.P., who took over the reins of office, and would have made Southport a name in the Football world had Southport people ever understood the value of a Soccer Club, and manifested a desire for progress in the football world.

In war-time football to popularize the Club, they pinned on the Club name as part and parcel of it, the title " Vulcan,"  To put it bluntly the Club, which was never a works Club, sold itself to public opinion to ensure sufficient funds to keep the Club going.  It could only be a temporary expedient, for the title must eventually wound the pride of the aristocratic population of this beauty resort on the Lancashire Coast.

When the Northern Section of the League was formed, Mr. Clayton, who is imbued with the aspirations of the town, possibly because he was a Member of the Town Council, took an active, one might say a leading part, in the formation of the Section, and whilst Alderman Cropper, of Chesterfield, was their spokesman and special pleader, Mr. Clayton was buttonholing the Clubs, and presenting his case to the few, knowing that the essential to success was votes.

With promotion came responsibility.  The ground was converted into one of reasonable proportions and enjoyable surroundings.  An adequate grand stand was erected, and a covered shelter provided for the spectators who could not afford to pay Stand prices.  Now the time has arrived when Southport must win friends by results rather than promises.  In Cup Competitions they have had their proud successes, as Burnley and Blackburn Rovers can testify.  For long years the Club has been content to rely on Honorary Officials, and those who have had to run foot-

SOUTHPORT F.C.

WINNERS OF LANCASHIRE CUP, 1904-05.

Back Row: S. Rigby (Trainer), F. Spink, F. Dent, J. Rimmer.
Middle Row: J. Sinclair, S. Smith, F. Chorlton, T. Edmonds.
Front Row: —. Dawson, J. Shadbolt, —. Lawson, H. Danson.

ball in their spare time. They made a plunge in appointing Mr. Tom Maley as Manager, but results proved that they would be better advised to be more modest, and now Mr. Charles Parker is installed as Secretary-Manager. Can he bring some of the glory of his old Club, Preston North End, to Southport? Time alone can tell. It is worth the effort, for Southport is much too proud to be satisfied with anything but the best.

The present Chairman is Mr. G. F. M. Moore, and the Secretary, Mr. Chas. Parker.

The Club has passed through the following stages :—
Southport Central, 1888.
Southport Wanderers, 1894.
Southport Central, 1895.
Southport Vulcan (during War time football).
Southport, on entering the Third Division.

The Club's first President was the late Mr. Isaac Smith who for many years served on the Lancashire F.A. Council.

## WIGAN BOROUGH, F.C.

Wigan, the sport of every comedian, yet a centre of great advantage, not merely to Lancashire, but to the whole world, is known mainly for its coal. The town boasts two Rugby League Clubs, but there are amongst its sport-loving population a few men who believe in Soccer football, and have made many sacrifices to build up an Association Club worthy of the town. They have tried and failed, and tried again. With failure has come a greater determination to succeed. Let it be said that the battle to establish a League Club has been a grim fight against greater odds and stronger opposition than most people imagine. Determination has been their watchword, and in the end the Directors will win through. The Rugby people did not take kindly to the introduction of the Association game. and those interested in the latter felt very keenly the determination of the Rugby Clubs to prevent them making friends.

You may put back the hands of the clock, but you do not alter the time. You may boom and subsidise a rival code, but you cannot smother the growth and attraction of Soccer. The boys loved the game, for they were happy in the constant use of their feet, they had joy in heading a ball which would carry true, and on all sides this incessant cry for Soccer was heard. When Mr. Alec Young and his brother, the brothers Culshaw, Mr. John Heaton, and a few others, said, Wigan Borough must become a live force in the game, they set the desires of many people aflame, but, alas, like others, they thought they could start at the top instead of striving to build up from the bottom. You cannot establish Clubs in some centres as easily as did Bradford City, Bradford, Huddersfield Town and Leeds United. Rome was not built in a day, and if Wigan Borough had been content to follow in the footsteps of Aston Villa and Everton, Oldham Athletic and Blackpool, they would have known that great endings had evolved from small beginnings. Perhaps by this they have also found out that it is a mistaken policy for a young and ambitious Club to trust in names, and pin their faith on players going off, rather than in players coming on.

The work and responsibility has been carried on by few, and though they struck on ambitious lines engaging Mr. H. S. Bamlett as Manager, they found that it was wise to creep and then walk before they tried to run. Some day they will run well, and instead of being classed amongst the also rans, they will get a place, then football will boom, and Soccer will come into its own. As yet it may be said, " They have won nothing." That is not true. They have won friends and gained experience, both of which will help them for the future.

The Club was formed in November, 1920, taking over the fixtures of the now defunct Wigan United in the Lancashire Combination, and was elected to the 3rd Division (Northern Section) of The Football League in March, 1921.

# CHAPTER XXXI.

## PRIMARY SCHOOL FOOTBALL IN LANCASHIRE.

### By J. Twist, Hon. Secretary.

*Schoolboy Football. The following chapter is not merely a record of work done, but is inserted by the compilers of the Jubilee History in appreciation of the great work so willingly performed by Mr. J. Twist, the Hon Secretary of the Schoolboys' Association, and his many colleagues.*

Whatever period may have seen the birth of the game of football, schoolboy football can probably boast of an equally hoary antiquity, for while the child is father to the man, whatever pursuits the man follows in athletic contests, the boy will emulate.

It is probably due, indeed, to the schools that our present-day popularity of football be ascribed. Medieval football was popular among the masses until the end of the 17th century when it declined considerably in public favour. Despite this, the great public schools of Eton, Harrow, Rugby, Winchester, Westminster, and Charterhouse, continued to play the game within their respective foundations.

When the revival of interest in the game came about in the nineteenth century, this was largely due to the influence and efforts of old Etonians, Harrovians, and other past scholars of the older public schools.

Early records of football in Lancashire go back into the good old days of " Merrie England," and the lads of Lancashire have probably played as long as their seniors.

As regards organised inter-school football, Lancashire school-masters have long claimed to have been the pioneers in fostering interest in football in the elementary schools. Their claim has not yet been contested.

**SCHOOLBOYS' CUP.**
Provided by Lancashire F.A. for approved Competitions.
(See Page 229).

Manchester Schools' Athletic Association was founded at the instigation of the late Mr. George Sharples in 1889, and at the outset was purely a football organisation. In the earlier years of football activities, Stretford, Salford, and Prestwich, were parts of the parent body, but now these thriving offshoots are strong enough in themselves to challenge the city supremacy in the national and county competitions. Even in the early days, long before the English Schools' Football Association was thought of, representative games were played.

School football was played in Liverpool in the Seventies of last century, but definite records of inter-school competitions date from 1893, in which year Aigburth National School won the senior football competition.

The first meeting convened to form what was known as Bolton and District Elementary Schools' Athletic Association was called by Mr. M. T. Morris, 5th November, 1898, at Hamer's Temperance Hotel, Bolton. A peculiar fact is that Committee Meetings and Annual Meetings have been held there ever since. Lord Stanley (afterwards the present Earl of Derby) presented them with a handsome bronze trophy known as The Stanley Shield.

The late Alderman Ord, a member of The F.A. and the L.F.A., gave to the Preston Schools' Association a cup for Annual Competition. Ever since 1906 the final for the Ord Cup has been played at Deepdale, the home of the Preston North End.

The Harry Boyle Cup will ever be remembered as the trophy which gave the impetus to the football activities of the Blackburn Schools' Football.

In 1904 the English Schools' Football Association was formed with 21 affiliated towns. Of these no fewer than 6 (Bolton, Bury, Darwen, Liverpool, Lancaster, Manchester), were from Lancashire. From these small beginnings the

Schoolboy National Competition now attracts nearly three
hundred town associations, some thirty of these being from
the Red-Rose County.

But participation in the All-England Competition has
not always been financially successful to the smaller towns,
where big ' gates ' are not available, and the founding of a
County Competition has been a useful and successful compromise.

Lancashire Schoolboy Football emerged from a parochial state to one of importance with the birth of the Lancashire County Elementary Schools' Football Association.
This was the outcome of a meeting called by the writer at
the suggestion of the late Mr. John Lewis, President of the
Lancashire Football Association, which met at the L.F.A.
offices, then in Ainsworth Street, Blackburn, 2nd January,
1920. Representatives were present from Barrow-in-Fur-
ness, Bolton, Burnley, Blackburn, Chorley, Liverpool,
Great Harwood, Manchester, Preston. Provisional rules
were framed, and a Cup Competition for which the Lancashire Football Association gave a Silver Cup, decided
upon. Seven towns only (Barrow, Blackburn, Bolton,
Burnley, Liverpool, Manchester and Preston) took part in
the Competition in its first season. From this humble beginning the Association has gone on increasing in strength.
The returns for Season 1926-27 show 50 affiliated
associations representing upwards of 1,000 Schools. It
has to be recorded that in addition to giving the Cup, the
L.F.A. present beautiful medals suitably inscribed to the
finalists.

The Lancashire Schools Association is truly a corporate
body, and undoubtedly it is a worthy force in the area of
its operation. The Game : its interests and the achievement of its practice in healthy exercise, with the development of the essence of good sportsmanship, are the objects
modestly pursued by the Lancashire Schoolboys' Football
Association.

To further foster and encourage Football among the Schoolboys of the Elementary Schools, the Lancashire Football Association has presented Cups to the following Schools Associations.

Atherton Schools F.A., 1927.
Barrow Schools F.A. 1920.
Hindley Schools F.A., 1923.
Lancaster Schools F.A., 1922.
Leigh and District Schools F.A., 1922.
Makerfield Schools F.A., 1925.
Preston Schools F.A., 1923.
West Lancashire Schools, Rural Area, 1928.

The Winners and Runners-up for the Lancashire County Elementary Schools F.A. Cup, are as follows :—

|         |     | WINNERS.    | RUNNERS-UP.       |
|---------|-----|-------------|-------------------|
| 1919-20 | ... | BOLTON      | SALFORD           |
| 1920-21 | ... | MANCHESTER  | BARROW-IN-FURNESS |
| 1921-22 | ... | MANCHESTER  | BURNLEY           |
| 1922-23 | ... | BLACKBURN   | ECCLES            |
| 1923-24 | ... | BOLTON      | MANCHESTER        |
| 1924-25 | ... | MANCHESTER  | LIVERPOOL         |
| 1925-26 | ... | LIVERPOOL   | BLACKBURN         |
| 1926-27 | ... | MANCHESTER  | LIVERPOOL         |
| 1927-28 | ... | LIVERPOOL   | MANCHESTER        |

RICHARD BIRTWISTLE.
Life Member of Lancashire F.A.

# CHAPTER XXXII.

## OFFICERS OF THE LANCASHIRE F.A.

*This Chapter and succeeding ones contain " Tabloid Biographies of Members of Lancashire F.A. Council :—R. Birtwistle, Life Member; T. Laithwaite, Hon. Treasurer; E Little, R. E. Lythgoe, J. McKenna, T. Y. Ritson, and R. Watson, Vice-Presidents.*

## R. BIRTWISTLE.

He attended the first Meeting of the Association, and served on the L.F.A. in 1879-80. He resumed his connection in 1901, was elected a Vice-President in 1919, and received his Long Service Medal in 1921. Mr. Birtwistle played with Blackburn Rovers in its early days, and later served the Club as Committeeman, Director and Chairman. He attended The F.A. Cup Final in 1881-82, since which he has attended every Final Tie. No representative match would be complete without " Dick " Birtwistle, and there is no man with so complete a knowledge of the history of the game, of its rise and development.

Mr. Birtwistle is generally a man of few words, though the latter generally convey a world of meaning. He played with Turton, Cob Wall, and Blackburn Rovers, and remembers the days when tape was used for the " crossbar."

Mr. Birtwistle resigned through failing health on June 23rd, 1927, and he was then elected a Life Member of the Association.

On August 17th, 1927, Mr. Birtwistle was presented with a Silver Casket in recognition of his long service to the Association.

## T. LAITHWAITE.

Elected to L.F.A. Council in 1904. In 1903 he missed election by one vote. Received his Long Service Medal in 1925; elected Vice-Chairman of the Referees' Committee in 1920, and succeeded Mr. C. E. Sutcliffe as Chairman in 1926.

No one has worked harder for Junior football, and Lancashire football in general. Constant in attendance at Meetings and enthusiastic in all his efforts. Member of Amateur Cup Committee and Discipline Committee. Was a Referee for many years, and refereed in many important matches.

He was honoured with the following appointments :—
Referee in The F.A. Amateur Cup Final Tie, 1912-13. Referee in the Lancashire Junior Cup Final Tie, 1905-6 and 1906-7, and refereed the Lancashire Amateur Cup Final Tie in 1909-10; and for a number of years he was a Football League Linesman.

He is known as "the Mayor of Wigan," and is a universal provider of mirth.

On June 23rd, 1927, Mr. Laithwaite succeeded Mr. Little as Hon. Treasurer, and thereby secured well-deserved recognition of twenty-three years' service as a Divisional member.

Mr. Laithwaite takes 100 per cent. interest in Junior and Amateur Football. "His Worship" is a Life President of the Lancashire Alliance and of the Wigan Cup Competition, and he is connected with every league in and around Wigan.

## E. LITTLE.

Elected to represent Division 6 in 1904. Received his Long Service Medal in 1925 and elected Hon. Treasurer in 1926, when Mr. Ritson vacated the position to become a Vice-President, and in turn, vacated the position of Hon. Treasurer to become a Vice-President on June 23rd, 1927.

Mr. Little was elected Chairman of the Leagues Sanction Committee in 1910, and has been most painstaking in this most difficult part of the Asociation's work. (See the Chapter on Leagues Sanction Committee).

He has served as a Director of the Blackpool F.C., and is President of the Fylde League ; and also President of the Fylde Referees' Society; he is also Chairman of Discipline Meetings held at Preston.

Mr. Little has not only rendered faithful service to the Association, but his sympathies have been extensive, as, for example, his connection with Penrith F.C., of which he has been a Vice-President for over twenty years.

He is a man of sound judgment, his strength being in his loyalty to his colleagues, and in his generosity and kindness to all.

## R. E. LYTHGOE.

Mr. Lythgoe was elected to represent Division 5 of the Lancashire F.A. in 1892, and received his Long Service Medal in 1913, and was elected a Vice-President in 1922.

He is one of the oldest men connected with official football, and played in goal for West Druids F.C., and was Secretary for that Club so far back as 1874. In 1877 he settled in Liverpool and became connected with the Birkenhead and Bootle Clubs. He also helped to form the Liverpool F.A. in 1882.

Mr. Lythgoe is affectionately referred to as " Bobby," and is held in high esteem by his Colleagues.

He was elected to the Council of The F.A. so long ago as 1884, and was elected a Vice-President in 1926. He further was the Hon. Secretary of the Liverpool County F.A. for many years, and is now its Hon. Treasurer.

Mr. Lythgoe, though 79 years of age, retains a delightful cheerfulness, and his interest in the game is as keen as ever, and he still retains the position of Secretary to Division 2 of The F.A., whose functions are the drawing of Clubs, arrangements for replays, and the appointment of Officials for the Qualifying Rounds of The F.A. Cup Competition.

Mr. Lythgoe was for many years one of our leading Referees, having refereed several International Matches, and also officiated as Linesman in three F.A. Cup Final Ties.   He also officiated at the historic Kennington Oval, and he acted as Linesman at the first Lancashire Cup Final Tie played between Darwen and Blackburn Rovers in 1879.

Mr. Lythgoe is a Member of the L.F.A. Finance and Referees' Committees.

## J.  McKENNA.

Mr. McKenna needs little introduction. his name being known throughout the land.

He was elected to represent Division 5 on the Lanca·shire Football Asociation in 1899, received his Long Service Medal in 1920. and was made a Vice-President in 1918. In 1909-10 he was Chairman of the Leagues Sanction Committee, and now holds a similar position on The Football Association.

Mr. McKenna was elected a Member of The Football Association Council in 1905, and was elected a Vice-President in 1912, he also became a Member of The Football League Management Committee in May, 1902, was made a Vice-President in 1908, and became President of that great Organisation in 1910, which position he still so worthily holds, and in 1923 he was elected a Life Member, when also he was presented with a silver-gilt casket containing an illuminated address.

Mr. McKenna has also served as Director, and Chairman of Directors, of the Liverpool F.C., and his extensive experience has been of great service to the County Association, especially during the period of reconstruction at the close of the Great War.

Few men have given so much time and service to the game as Mr. McKenna.  His genial wit, coupled with his keen love for the game has made him popular whereever football is played.   The Liverpool F.C. is very largely what he made it, for through all its trials he was a faithful friend and adviser. His opinions are always carefully considered, and his sound judgment universally respected and accepted. His honesty and business aptitude is such that he cannot tolerate any malpractice or laxity of method. At times he is severe almost to the point of harshness, but his sternest moments always end with kindly good humour. As a Vice-President of The Football Association he is respected equally with the President.

## T. Y. RITSON.

Elected in 1901 to represent Division III., and received his Long Service Medal in 1922. In 1915 he was appointed Hon. Treasurer, and in 1926 he was made a Vice-President.

Mr. Ritson has rendered long and faithful service to the Association. He first played " Rugger " at school, but later joined Bolton Christ Church and played " Soccer " with them in all positions. He played one year with Christ Church F.C., and that was the last year the club was so called. The Club then changed its name to Bolton Wanderers. Mr. Ritson next played with Mawdsley F.C. Later, Mr. Ritson, along with several other ex-Rugby players, then formed the Bolton and District F.A., and amongst the members were G. Dobson (afterwards a player of Bolton Wanderers and Everton), Joe Sowerbutts (who later played with Blackburn Rovers), and W. Flitcroft (who became a Bolton Wanderer).

Mr. Ritson was one of the first dozen to take up shares when the Wanderers Club was made into a Limited Company, he was also the first Shareholders' Auditor, and later became a Director of the Club, and when the Club was short of a Secretary he acted as Hon. Secretary. Mr. Ritson was Chairman of the Club during the last three or four years that he was a Director, from which position he resigned in 1904.

The activities of Mr. Ritson on behalf of The Lancashire F.A. have been manifold.  He is a Member of the
Finance, Referees, and Discipline Committees, and he is
Chairman of the Jubilee Banquet Committee, and if zeal
and energy can ensure success, then the Association's
celebrations will be of the best.

## R.  WATSON.

Elected to represent Division I. in 1892.  Received his
Long Service Medal in 1913, and made a Vice-President in
1918.

Mr. Watson has over 40 years  connection  with the
game, he was connected with Bells' Temperance, later
connected with Accrington and Accrington Stanley.

For many years was a Football League Linesman and
Combination Referee.  Was Linesman in The F.A. Cup
Final Tie at Crystal Palace in 1909-10, and also in the Re-
play at Everton, when Newcastle United  beat  Barnsley
2—0, after a Draw of 1—1, he was also Linesman in the
Inter-League match, England v. Scotland, played at Ewood
Park in 1909-10.  Mr. Watson holds two records, having
been the Referee in 6 Lancashire Junior Cup Final Ties,
and in 4 Amateur Cup Final Ties.

Mr. Watson is generally referred to as "Dick," and
his name is a household word in Accrington, where he
lives, and is a member of the Town Council.  He is
President of the North-East Lancashire Combination,
Chairman of the Lancashire Combination Executive,
President of Blackburn and District Referees' Society, and
also represents Division II. on the Council of The F.A.,
and yet finds time for his Sunday School and Social work,
and in connection with the latter he is proud of a medal
presented to him for twenty-one years' continuous service.

Mr. Watson is Chairman of the Discipline Committee
of the L.F.A., and also serves on the Finance, Referees,
Rules Revision, and Jubilee Committees, and his attendance at these and other football meetings are as the wine
of life to him.

# CHAPTER XXXIII.

## MEMBERS OF THE LANCASHIRE F.A. COUNCIL.

### TABLOID BIOGRAPHIES—*continued*.

*T. A. Barcroft, R. A. Beeley, W. E. Bracewell, T. P. Campbell, E. Clayton, J.P., W. Dickinson, H. Duckworth, C. E. Foweraker, H. P. Hardman, and J. W. Haworth.*

## T. A. BARCROFT.

Mr. Barcroft was elected a Divisional Member for Division 6 in 1912, in succession to the late Tom Houghton.

Mr. Barcroft's connection with Blackpool F.C. is known world wide, and an appropriate telegraphic address would be " cheerio " or " smile."

Mr. Barcroft is a Member of The Football League and also Treasurer of the Central League, and he has on several occasions unsuccessfully sought election on The F.A. He is a Member of the L.F.A. Referees' Committee and Discipline Committee, and amongst his various characteristics he possesses a fund of anecdotes, which he relates inimicably.

He is not only Hon. Secretary of the Blackpool F.C., but he is the only Hon. Secretary of any Club connected with The Football League. Football is his only hobby, on which he spends practically every hour of the day.

## R. A. BEELEY.

Elected to the Council in 1925.

Mr. Beeley is a Director of Lancaster Town F.C., he is also a Member of the Lancashire Combination Executive, and also connected with the North Lancashire League.

Though young in service with the Lancashire F.A., Mr. Beeley has shown a willingness to respond to the confidence reposed in him, and as one of the younger Members he ought to have a long career of service.

Q

**BLACKBURN CROSS HILL A.F.C.**

WINNERS OF LANCASHIRE AMATEUR CUP, 1902-3.

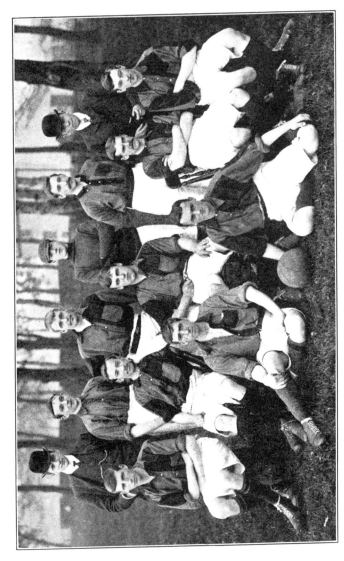

F. Cunliffe (Hon. Treasurer), H. Slater (Captain), W. Marsh, G. F. Clarke, Dr. Leighton, H. H. Birtwistle (Hon. Secretary). W. Crabtree, J. Garstange, S. Heaton, W. Cooper, A. Dawson, W. Neville, H. Woolfall.

# W. E. BRACEWELL.

Elected in 1919 for Division I., two months after the election of his Club Colleague, Mr. H. Windle.

It is said that apart from football Mr. Bracewell's chief hobby is " leg pulling," at which he is a past master.

As a football " scout " he has done invaluable service and amongst the " stars " whom he helped to secure for Burnley were " Bob " Kelly, Sewell, Jones and Waterfield.

Mr. Bracewell is a Director of Burnley F.C., having been associated with the Club for over thirty years, his first connection being that of a Junior Clerk in the office. He serves on the L.F.A. Rules Revision, Discipline, and Permits Committees, and his services for and on behalf of Junior Football have been very helpful. He is also a Member of the Central League Management Committee, and Vice-Chairman of the North-East Lancashire Combination.

As evidence of his popularity, he has headed the poll at four elections in connection with the election of Directors for Burnley F.C., which Board he joined in 1909, and of which he is Chairman of the Finance Committee, he is also a Vice-President of the Burnley Referees Society and of the Burnley Sunday School Football League.

# T. P. CAMPBELL.

Mr. Campbell—often referred to as " T.P.," commenced his football career with Brae Side F.C., later he played with Blackburn Park Road F.C. He was, of course, always an amateur player, but some of his colleagues were professionals and received the princely sum of 2/6 per week.

" T.P." assisted Blackburn Rovers F.C. on several occasions, and played for the famous Club v. Glasgow Rangers on the Leamington ground, he also played against Preston North End when the Rovers won by many goals.

On three occasions Mr. Campbell was selected to represent
Blackburn and District against other Lancashire Districts,
and that was no little honour in those days.

A broken knee cap terminated T.P.'s " career as a
football player, and thereafter his energies were directed
in acting as Referee and in Committee work. For many
years Mr. Campbell was a Lancashire Combination and a
Football League Referee. In 1907-08 he refereed the Lancashire Cup Final Tie when Oldham Athletic beat Preston
North End by three goals to one at Hyde Road, and the
same Season he had the great honour of refereeing The
F.A. Cup Final Tie when Wolverhampton Wanderers beat
Newcastle United by three goals to one at the Crystal
Palace.

Mr. Campbell is now President of the Lancashire Combination, having served on the Committee for several
years. He is also President of Blackburn and District
Combination, with which he was actively connected for
over 21 years. He is also Hon. Secretary of the East
Lancashire Charity Committee, which is one of the oldest
Competitions in Lancashire.

" T.P." was elected a Member of the L.F.A. Council
in 1914, and has rendered yeoman service on the Amateur,
Discipline, Referees, and League's Sanction Committees.
He is also a Member of the Jubilee Banquet Committee.
Mr. Campbell, it is said, is equally good at leg pulling, playing bowls and coon-can, watching cricket, criticising present day football and footballers, or in " yarn spinning."

He has just been appointed Chairman of the Amateur
Cup Committee, in succession to Mr. C. E. Sutcliffe, who
retired from that position in 1928.


## E. CLAYTON, J.P.

Elected in 1924 for Division 5, his interests are mani-
fold, having been a Member of the Southport
Town Council for many years; but Southport
F.C. has always claimed a large share of Mr.
Clayton's time and support, of which he was Secretary for

many years. In 1926 he was elected on the Lancashire Combination Executive. Mr. Clayton serves on the L.F.A. Referees and Discipline Committees, and his comprehensive experience of men and matters are of great service to the Association.

Mr. Clayton takes an active part in the Civic life of Southport, and in August, 1927, was appointed a Justice of the Peace.

He took a great interest in the promotion of the Northern Section, Third Division, of The Football League, and is ever on the alert to further the interests of the Clubs concerned.

## W. DICKINSON.

Mr. Dickinson was one of the Referees whose name appeared on the first list in 1901, when registration of Referees was etablished. He was a Football League Linesman, and a Referee in the North-Eastern League, and Lancashire Combination.

Elected on L.F.A. Council in 1915, has been connected with Furness F.A. and North-Western League for many years, also the Barrow F.C. as Director, Chairman, Vice-Chairman and Secretary.

Mr. Dickinson in representing the Barrow area has to travel more than any other Member of the Council in attending the Council Meetings.

Mr. Dickinson has experienced every phase of football, and his services are of great help in the Northern corner of the County.

## H. DUCKWORTH.

Elected for Division 4 in 1923, a worthy son of a worthy sire, his father, the late W. A. Duckworth, having been a Member of the Council from 1892 to 1918.

Like his father, Mr. Duckworth is keenly interested in football, and Bury F.C. in particular.

Mr. Duckworth was elected Vice-Chairman of the Referees' Committee in 1926, and is also a Member of the Leagues Sanction Committee, Discipline Committee, and Jubilee History Committee.

**EARLE F.C.**

WINNERS OF AMATEUR CUP, 1926-27.

A. Littler (Committee), F. O. Hesketh, J. D. Handley, A. Threlfall, E. F. Adams, R. Fairfoul, O. H. Paulsen, A. R. Holland,
  G. Bennison (Hon. Sec.), A. Dadswell (Chairman).
Seated : F. G. Brewer, R. W. Henshall, E. J. Pollock, W. L. Sansbury, A. W. Childs, H. Wilkins, W. Metcalf (Trainer).

Mr. Duckworth is also President of the Bury Referees' Society, is a Member of Manchester F.A. Council, and last —but certainly not least—he is the Chairman of Bury F.C.

## C. E. FOWERAKER.

Mr. Foweraker was appointed Manager to Bolton Wanderers F.C. in July, 1919, prior to which he had served the Club in different capacities.

Mr. Foweraker, is, needless to state, well known in football circles, yet it is not long since he had the unique experience of being refused admission to his own ground, thanks to the zeal of a new checker who did not know him, and only the timely intervention of the President of the Lancashire F.A. saved the situation.

He was elected to represent Division 3 in 1922.

Mr. Foweraker as Secretary-Manager of Bolton Wanderers F.C. has seen his Club capture The F.A. Cup in 1923 and 1926, and the scenes in the 1923 Final will never be forgotten. His connection with the Lancashire F.A. has cemented the good feeling between the Association and its Professional Clubs. He is a Member of the League's Sanction, Referees', Discipline, and Jubilee Match Committees, and his tact, experience, and sound judgment have been, and are, of great service.

## H. P. HARDMAN.

Elected to the Council in June, 1928, after unsuccessful attempts in 1925 and 1926.

Mr. Hardman first played football for Blackpool High School, and whilst at school played for Blackpool F.C., in the Second Division of The Football League. That was away back in 1900-01. He played with Blackpool F.C. for three seasons, and then from 1903-04 to 1907-08 played with Everton, and later played with Manchester United, Bradford City, and his last club was Stoke, with whom he played from 1910-13, when he retired from playing.

The first medal Mr. Hardman obtained in football was an English Cup medal, he being a member of the Everton team that beat Newcastle United 1—0 in 1905-06. His second medal was an English Cup runners-up medal received the following season when Sheffield Wednesday beat Everton by 2—0. Mr. Hardman not only played for England in English Amateur Internationals and Olympic Games, but he played with professionals in International Matches against Scotland in 1907, against Wales in 1905-08, and against Ireland in 1907.

Mr. Hardman was elected a Member of the Central League Committee in June, 1923, and still retains that office. He also became a Director of Manchester United in 1911. Amongst other clubs that he helped at different times were Northern Nomads, Worsley Wanderers, and Chorlton-cum-Hardy.

The first person to get Mr. Hardman interested in League football was Bob Birkett, who played for Blackpool, and who used to keenly watch School matches, and he and the late R. B. Middleton interviewed Mr. Hardman's father, and secured permission to sign him as an Amateur, so, after all, English Schools' football does provide opportunities for our boys to learn to shoot.


## J. W. HAWORTH.

Co-opted a Member of the Amateur Cup Committee in 1920, and in 1925 was co-opted a Member of the Council, as a representative of the Amateur Cup Clubs.

Mr. Haworth was connected with Stockport County F.C. thirty-eight years ago, and later he became associated with Heaton Chapel A.F.C., whom he has served for twenty-four years, and on some occasions he has been the " crowd " watching his Club. He has been, and is, also actively associated with the Lancashire Amateur League, of which he has been a Member eighteen years.

Mr. Haworth has one object, to see Amateur football flourish, and he is unsparing in his efforts on behalf of amateurs and amateurism.

# CHAPTER XXXIV.

## MEMBERS OF THE LANCASHIRE F.A. COUNCIL.

### TABLOID BIOGRAPHIES (CONTINUED).

*J. Kenny, J. E. Mangnall, F. Morris, E. A. Morton, J.P., W. J. Sawyer, J. Taylor, J. W. Walsh, H. Windle, E. C. Witter, J.P.*

## J. KENNY.

Mr. Kenny was co-opted to the Council in 1919, being the first member to be so appointed, and in 1926 was elected a Divisional Member (Division 6), and the same year was elected Vice-Chairman of the Leagues Sanction Committee; is also a Member of the Referees and Discipline Committees, and also of the Jubilee History and Jubilee Banquet Committees.

If Mr. Kenny, prior to his connection with the Lancashire F.A., was apprehensive of the " powers that be," he has probably had his doubts and fears dispelled. Mr. Kenny is President of the West Lancashire League, one of the oldest Leagues in the County, with which he has been connected over 21 years, and he is also President of the Preston and District Sunday School League. Mr. Kenny was a Football League Referee, refereed Lancashire Cup Final, Blackburn Rovers v. Burnley, in 1910-11, and was Linesman in the International Match at Liverpool in 1922, when England beat Wales by one goal to none. A man of determination and of set purpose.

## J. E. MANGNALL.

Mr. Mangnall was a Director of Bolton Wanderers at the time he became Secretary and Manager of Burnley F.C. He started with the latter on 1st January, 1900, and remained with the Club until October, 1903. He was then appointed Secretary-Manager to Manchester United, who were in the Second Division. In 1906 United gained promotion, and were Champions of the First Division in 1907-08 and 1910-11, and in 1908-09 they won The F.A. Cup. That is a great record and one for any Club to be proud of.

United left Clayton in 1911 and went to Old Trafford, with its palatial arrangements. In September, 1912, Mr. Mangnall left United and crossed over to the City. Mr. Mangnall remained with City until the end of Season 1923-24, during which time the Club removed from the popular but barren ground at Ardwick to Maine Road, with its huge resources.

Years ago Mr. Mangnall was a prominent athlete, and on the old ordinary cycle, cycled from Bolton to John-o'-Groats, and from John-o'-Groats to Land's End, and to-day holds all the records for Bolton and district for the 54 inch cycle. He won the long distance competition five years in succession. He was also Hon. Secretary of Bolton Harriers, and used to compete in Cross Country events and championships. Mr. Mangnall also took an active interest in boxing and swimming and won a number of trophies.

Whilst Mr. Mangnall has had an extensive career in the conduct and management of professional football, yet as a player he was an amateur, first playing Rugby and later Soccer, and he was always an amateur in the various athletics in which he engaged.

Mr. Mangnall joined The Lancashire F.A. in 1918, and is a Member of the League's Sanction, Referees, and Discipline Committees, he is Chairman and Treasurer of the Secretaries and Managers' Association, and is also on the Committee of Management of the Central League, of which he was a founder.

## F. MORRIS.

Elected in 1919 to represent Division 4, in succession to Mr. C. E. Sutcliffe, who had then been made a Vice-President.

Mr. Morris has for years been connected with the Radcliffe and District Sunday School League, one of the best controlled Junior Organisations in the County. He is a Member of the Leagues Sanction, Amateur Cup, Referees, and Discipline Committees, and gives a great amount of time and service to the Association.

Mr. Morris is a Member of the Radcliffe Urban District Council, and also holds high office in the Manchester Unity of Oddfellows.

## E. A. MORTON, J.P.

Mr. Morton was first connected with the Lancashire Football Association in 1893, when Hon. Secretary and Treasurer of the Old Xaverians A.F.C. He is a founder of the Lancashire I'Zingari League, and also of the Lancashire Amateur League. During the last four years, in conjunction with Mr. G. R. Mitchell (Liverpool Collegiate), he has established the Old Boys' League for Old Boys of Secondary Schools of Liverpool and District.

Mr. Morton has always kept in the closest touch with Amateur football, and he has always been a very loyal Member of the Lancashire F.A., and was first co-opted on the Council in October, 1921, as the representative of Amateur football.

Mr. Morton is a Life President of the Old Xaverians F.C., and in 1926 was appointed a Justice of the Peace for the City of Liverpool. He remembers the days when Amateur players who represented their County were called upon to pay their own expenses, even from Lancashire when visiting in the South of England, and he has also seen something of the struggles of Amateur Clubs to keep alive because of the great attractions of Professional football.

## MARINE A.F.C.
### AMATEUR CUP WINNERS, 1921-22

Inset: S. B. Berney (Secretary).

Standing: F. W. Lake (Team Manager), D. Alcock (Trainer), G. Day, L. Almond, W. Ross, J. H. Clayton, J. Smith (Asst. Trainer), F. W. Littleton (Hon. Secretary).

     F. Lomack, J. A. Warburton, W. McGowan (Captain), C. S. Haumaur, I. Davies, J. Jackson.

## W. J. SAWYER.

Mr. Sawyer was elected to the L.F.A. Council in 1921 in succession to the late Dr. Baxter, who had for several months represented Division 5.

Mr. Sawyer has a most extensive experience in football, as the following will indicate: Hon. Secretary of Everton F.C. in 1918, and in 1921 elected a Director of the Club, since which time he has been Chairman of the Finance Committee. His first connection with football was Hon. Secretary and Treasurer of the Leeds and Liverpool Canal Recreation, close on forty years ago. Prior to his joining Everton F.C. he was Secretary and Managing Director of South Liverpool F.C., now known as New Brighton F.C. He was also founder of the following organisations: Liverpool Mid-Week Hospital Cup Competition, South Liverpool F.C., Liverpool Football League, Wigan Borough F.C.

In addition to his work on the Council of the L.F.A., Mr. Sawyer is also connected with the Liverpool County F.A., of which he is a Vice-President. His connection with both professional and amateur football has been of service to the Lancashire F.A., and particularly the Amateur Cup Competition, as through his good offices several Final Ties have been played on the Everton and Liverpool grounds, and in that way Mr. Sawyer has shown a real and practical interest in amateur clubs.

## J. TAYLOR.

Elected to represent Division 3 in 1914, and is a Member of the Amateur Cup, Discipline, Leagues Sanction, Referees, and Jubilee Banquet Committees.

Mr. Taylor was an Amateur player for a number of years, later became President of Bolton and District A.F.A., and is most zealous in his efforts on behalf of Junior football, whilst the local Clubs all look to him as their friend.

In his younger days Mr. Taylor was a successful outside right, very speedy and clever, and he could easily have become a professional had he desired to do so. He played for his school at Lytham, and later played with Bolton Park Road F.C., Chequerbent F.C., and other Bolton Clubs.

Mr. Taylor was for some time a Member of the Bolton Town Council. Prior to the War he played Tennis, Bowls, Billiards, and Golf, and to-day takes an interest in all kinds of sport.

## J. W. WALSH.

Elected in 1925 for Division 2, Mr. Walsh is Chairman of the Blackburn Rovers F.C., and his predecessor on the L.F.A. was the late R. B. Middleton, Secretary of the Rovers.

As a Club Chairman Mr. Walsh knows something about the cares and difficulties of football management, and such experience will stand him in good stead on the L.F.A.

Was there a prouder man in England when the Rovers of 1928 won The F.A. Cup at Wembley, which great event was witnessed not only by His Majesty the King, but Queen Mary and the Duke and Duchess of York were also present?

Blackburn people showed their appreciation of the Rovers' triumph when the Team came home, and well may Mr. Walsh laugh and smile.

Mr. Walsh is a Member of the L.F.A. Referees, Discipline, and Rules Revision Committees. The Lancashire F.A. Council would, indeed, be strange without a Rovers official.

## H. WINDLE.

Elected to the Lancashire F.A. Council in April, 1919, for Division 1, and serves on the Discipline, League's Sanction, Referees and Jubilee Match Committees.

Mr. Windle was first connected with Burnley Lane Reform Club, and has always been interested in the administrative side of football. He is Chairman of the Burnley F.C., which position he has held for 19 years out of the 25 that he has been connected with that Club.

Mr. Windle's connection with the L.F.A. has strengthened the position of the latter, insomuch that the success of a County Association depends upon the co-operation and support of its Senior Clubs, and Mr. Windle's influence has been all to the good of the Lancashire F.A.

In 1927 Mr. Windle's admirers connected with Burnley F.C. presented him with a motor car in recognition of his interest and zeal on behalf of the Turf Moor Club and numerous local sports, including cricket.

Mr. Windle is also Hon. Treasurer of the Burnley Hospital Cup Competition, which is probably one of the biggest money-raising competitions in the country. Last season no less than £730 was paid over to the Burnley Hospital, a fact that Mr. Windle is very proud of, and the Hospital Committee also appreciate the fact that the Semi-Final and Final Ties are often successful because they are played on the ground of the Burnley F.C.

## E. C. WITTER, J.P.

Mr. Witter only became a Member of The Lancashire Association in 1927, succeeding Mr. T. Laithwaite, who had been promoted to the responsible post of Hon. Treasurer.

Mr. Witter, however, has for many years been a keen follower and supporter of football in general, and Junior and Amateur Football in particular. He is President of the Lancashire Alliance, to whom he gave a Cup, which is named the " Excelsior " Cup. He is also a Vice-President of Wigan Sunday School League, to whom he provided a Shield.

In his time Mr. Witter has been a player for Appley Bridge and other Clubs around the Wigan area. He is a Member of the Wigan Rural Council, and also is a County Justice of the Peace. His interest in sport is not confined to football, as he is President of a local Bowling Club, and also President of Appley Bridge Golf Club.

Mr. Witter should prove an acquisition to the Council.

**F. HARGREAVES,**
Secretary, Lancashire F.A.

# CHAPTER XXXV.

## OUR SECRETARY.
## MR. FRED HARGREAVES,

### By Chas. E. Sutcliffe.

Mr. Hargreaves is the present Secretary of the Association and the third since the formation of the Association. Starting with the Association as a youth he was soon entrusted with the work of the office under the supervision of Mr. R. P. Gregson, but in those days the Association was largely a close corporation, junior Clubs were neither encouraged nor desired, and the membership of the Association fell so low that the right of the Lancashire Football Association to representation on The Football Association was imperilled for lack of members. The Junior Clubs were regarded as a nuisance, and to govern them an undertaking which meant time, trouble, and expense. Even the registration and control of referees was an undertaking that the office was anxious to evade, and Mr. J. T. Howcroft was appointed Registrar.

The Council was not content to allow the Association to dwindle and decay, and ultimately determined to take control of all football, where Clubs were willing, or could be brought under the ægis of the Association. In appointing Mr. Hargreaves many people thought the Association had taken a risk, for he seemed so young to take upon his shoulders the Secretarial work of an Association of such importance, and carry through the schemes of extension which were then in their infancy, and which required very careful handling and much enthusiasm to see them through.

R

From the outset he has never failed to satisfactorily discharge the work of his office. Probably many County Associations feel happy in their chief working official, but there is none better fitted, more competent, and with a keener love for his work than the Secretary of the Lancashire F.A. Even during the War and whilst in the Army he carried on, and the work was never neglected nor did the Association suffer in his hands.

In the early days, he was perhaps fortunate in being in close touch and almost daily association with the late Mr. D. B. Woolfall, but from the time when he was called on to master all the rules and regulations and keep a keen supervision and control of the Association, he has grown in power and knowledge, until to-day he is looked up to as one of the leading authorities on the work and conduct of a County Association. Careful and methodical in all his work, the office system has been perfected by him, until the Association has become not merely his work or his hobby, but his life's work, in which to take a real pride.

There have been times when he has been tempted to take up other positions which would probably have been financially beneficial, and when the outlook seemed of wider scope, but he has always decided to remain at the work he loves and amongst a people that must now seem part of his life. Let me say quite frankly, that he must from time to time have found the policy and ideals, the whims and wishes of individual members of the Council, difficult to understand and dangerous to allow scope to. His powers of argument backed by his experience and unfailing tact have kept us from going astray so far as Rules and Regulations are concerned.

There must have been times when he would have been glad if he could have changed the President, for he was always a better Secretary than we conceived him to be, and it is not always easy to convince a President that he is wrong, but the time has never come when we have wished for another Secretary. Perhaps I write with greater freedom and force than could any other. I remember my own fears when the late Mr. Lewis left for Australia and I was called upon to take over the duty of Deputy-President. After my first chat with the Secretary all my fears vanished, and if Mr. Hargreaves was one half as happy under his added responsibility, as I was in trying to maintain the machinery of the Lancashire Football Association in its high state of efficiency, he was a happy man. When I returned the reins of office to Mr. Lewis I felt under a very great obligation to every member of the Council who had all the time striven to make my path easy and duties light, but when I passed out of the Presidential chair my heart was full of gratitude for the unvarying kindness and the very generous assistance the Secretary had shown and given me. Those few months enabled me to realise Mr. Hargreaves at his true worth.

I must say of him as I have written of our late President, that at times he has been obsessed with his own view as the only possible right view, but I love a tenacious fighter. We have failed to agree in our opinions and judgment, but we have always agreed as friends, and I hope better friends to-day because we had the courage to be frank, and the good sense never to be disagreeable. Since I took over the duties and responsibility of President, a position I regard as a very great honour, I have learned still more to appreciate the work of our Secretary, and to understand far better than I ever did before, the high esteem in which he holds the Association, the honour, dignity, and utility of which are safe in his hands. He is a model and faithful servant, but better still he is a real pal.

During his term of office the Association has grown by leaps and bounds, and the work increased to an amazing extent.

Mr. Hargreaves was for a number of years a Lancashire Combination and a Central League Referee, and also was Chairman of the Blackburn Thursday Amateur League for ten years; and he has for years taken an interest in the public life of Blackburn.

## LITTLE LEVER F.C.
### WINNERS OF JUNIOR SHIELD, 1926-27.

Back Row: R. Simms, G. Muncaster, G. Fairhurst.
Middle Row: J. Hatchman, W. Yates, H. Rothwell, W. Gardner, F. Ashworth.
Bottom Row: A. Ryder, J. Hurst, J. Cooper, G. S. Turner (Hon. Sec.), C. Cooper, F. Shard, S. Lever.

# CHAPTER XXXVI.

## IN HONOUR OF THE JUNIORS.

How delightful it would be to record the doings of all the Clubs in the County, but whilst the League Clubs are in everybody's mouth, the thousand and one Junior Clubs that have made football and football players are counted of no moment.

At this time when the big Clubs take pride in their greatness let them recall their earlier days. Let them also take stock of their players. Whence came they. Footballers have not learned the game on Ewood Park, Goodison Park, Deepdale and Old Trafford. On the grounds of Turton, Hindley, Black Lane, Atherton, Westhoughton and Little Lever, and in the ranks of Amateur Clubs, clubs' players have learned the game and learned to love it. In the days of their youth their enthusiasm has carried them on until they could not be content until they became masters of their profession.

The Junior Clubs are making, training, and coaching. Then as the players progress, the Clubs say, " We have finished our work, we have fitted you to perform before your tens and scores of thousands. Go, and our blessing goes with you, but remember that though you make your name with another Club, help to win Cups and Medals, and receive International honours, some of the credit belongs to us."

On June 23rd, 1928, just as we are revising the previous chapters of this book, the welcome intelligence is received that Turton F.C. (previously referred to as " defunct ") has " returned to life." This resuscitation of the old Club on the eve of the Association's Jubilee is a most happy event, and it is also worthy of note that the Secretary of the old Club is Mr. J. W. Howarth, a son of the late John James Howarth, who did so much for Junior football.

May the revival of Turton F.C. be a portent of a revival of interest in Junior and village football.

It is likewise impossible to portray the work and efforts and characteristics of the seventy leagues and competitions, but in the following chapters we include two contributions, one representative of Junior professional football, and the other having reference to a purely amateur and junior league, and each controlled in a manner commendable to all concerned.

# CHAPTER XXXVII.

## THE FYLDE DISTRICT FOOTBALL LEAGUE.

### By B. C. PLATT, HON. SECRETARY.

The first Meeting was held in the Marton Institute on August 22nd, 1898, and it was called by J. Rogers of South Shore.

On the proposition of W. Marquis, of Wesham, seconded by W. Marshal, of Freckleton, it was decided to form a Football League, to be called the Fylde District Amateur Football League.

The League has carried on ever since (except for the War period 1914-1919) and to-day has two Divisions with 26 Clubs in Membership, who compete for the following trophies : 1st Division Championship, "The Bannister Cup," presented by the late Thomas Bannister, President in 1889-90 and 1890-91 ; the 2nd Division Championship, "The John Gaunt Cup," presented by John Gaunt ; also for the 1st Division teams the Fylde League Challenge Cup, presented by Saul Shiers, who was President in 1901-02; for the 2nd Division teams, The Ramsden Challenge Shield, presented by Charles Ramsden, President in 1903-04.

The League is noted for the long service of its Officials, as the following list will show.

On December 6th, 1926, the League honoured the following ten gentlemen by electing them the first " life members " of the League. They were each presented with an illuminated scroll.

President, Edward Little, 23 years' service to the League.

Chairman, Albert Hargreaves, 29 years' service to the League.

Vice-Chairman, Arthur Ward, 24 years' service to the League.

Fred Birtwistle, 27 years' service to the League.

Vice-President, Adam Atkinson, 24 years' service to the League.

John Gaunt, 20 years' service to the League.

Vice-President, William McCaffery, 26 years' service to the League.

Vice-President, Thomas A. Barcroft, 18 years' service to the League.

Vice-President, Charles Ramsden, 24 years' service to the League.

Albert Briggs, 17 years' service to the League.

Of the old Clubs, Wesham and South Shore are still Members, whilst Freckleton only dropped out at the end of last Season, owing to having lost their ground. The present 1st Division Champions, the Alkali Works F.C., won their first Championship after 20 years' effort. The Alkali Works have the finest sports ground in the League.

The Lytham Institute were the first Champions in 1899. South Shore hold the record as Champions, being at the top of the 1st Division from 1919 to 1923.

Freckleton, Fleetwood Amateurs, and Blackpool Athletic have all been three times Champions. In the 2nd Division, formed in 1920, no team has yet been twice the Champions.

In the "Fylde Cup" Blackpool Athletic hold the record, they have been holders four times.

" The Ramsden Shield " has only been won on two occasions by one Club, Fleetwood Wednesday.

The League has turned out four of the finest Internationals who have played for England, Jack Cox (of Blackpool and Liverpool), Harold Hardman, Joe McCall, and George Wilson, whilst other Internationals, Herbert Jones and M. Webster (of Middlesbro) also played in the Fylde League.

Besides serving the League Mr. Little is also President of the Fylde Referees' Society, and is a very " live President "; he is always looking after the interests of its Members.

## CROSTON F.C.
### WINNERS OF JUNIOR CUP, 1922-23.

Back Row: J. Taylor, S. Vickers, C. Livesey.

Second Row: A. T. Alty, J. Almond, R. Almond, W. Aspinall, P. Sharples, H. Cook, T. Tuson, R. Whittle, R. Tuson (Trainer).

Front Row: J. Tunstall, T. Houghton, J. Halshaw, J. Sumner, J. Spencer, —. Gornall, J. W. Yates.

## THE WEST LANCASHIRE LEAGUE.

### By A. WARD, HON. SECRETARY.

This League was originally named "The Preston and District Football Combination," being formed in season 1905-6, and ran for three Seasons under that name, when, owing to the fact that the Clubs comprising the competition covered a bigger area, and to avoid clashing with another organisation, the present title was adopted.

The original clubs were thirteen in number, and Coppull Central had the honour of being first champions, and the Club maintained an unbroken membership of the League up to the close of season 1925-26, when, owing to the coal dispute and financial troubles, they were compelled to withdraw, so that not one of the original clubs remain members. So far as the officials were concerned, however, four members who were present at the formation are still actively identified, and have served the League faithfully and well throughout, these being the President, Mr. John Kenny; Chairman, Mr. Walter Archer, and two Members of the Committee, Messrs. Robert Armstrong and Albert Haworth. As these gentlemen had given 21 years' service the League took the opportunity at a Coming of Age Dinner, held at Preston on March 22nd, 1927, to make suitable presentations in recognition and also to celebrate the League's Coming of Age.

This was attended by Members of The Lancashire Football Association, The Football League, The Lancashire Combination, and other kindred bodies, and proved a huge success.

Notable feats by Clubs are that of Croston F.C. in winning the Lancashire Junior Cup in Season 1922-23, and Lytham F.C.'s great performance of going right through the Football Association's Cup qualifying rounds, to the Competition proper, in Season 1925-26, to be beaten by Oldham Athletic, a Football League Club, in the first round.

Breightmet United in their first season also put up a record by winning the League Championship, Richardson Cup and West Lancashire League Cup in Season 1926-27.

The League has met with some serious rebuffs at various times, and had to search for clubs as members, but the storms have all been weathered, and a record number of clubs, *i.e.* 16, covering all parts of the County, is now assured, and as the financial position is a good one, a period of prosperity is looked for.

It has been suggested that the present title is a misnomer, but for old association, sentimental reasons, and the fact that the dropping of the word " West " would cause a similarity of names with other organisations in the County, no change is contemplated at present.

The League values highly the fact that its President, Mr. John Kenny, was honoured by the Lancashire Football Association in being co-opted a Member of its Council in 1919 and still retains the confidence of that organisation.

**PRESTON WINCKLEY A.F.C.**

AMATEUR CUP WINNERS, 1907-08.

Second Row: R. Margerison (Committee), A. G. R. Rigby (Secretary), R. L. Taylor, J. Winchester, F. Ward, G. Margerison, P. Grime, S. Whitehead (Treasurer), F. Brandwood (Joint Secretary).
Front Row: W. Sharples, J. Haworth, E. Mansfield, B. Berry (Captain), W. Hodgson, J. E. Hothersall.

**WIGAN AMATEURS F.C.**

AMATEUR CUP WINNERS, 1909-10.

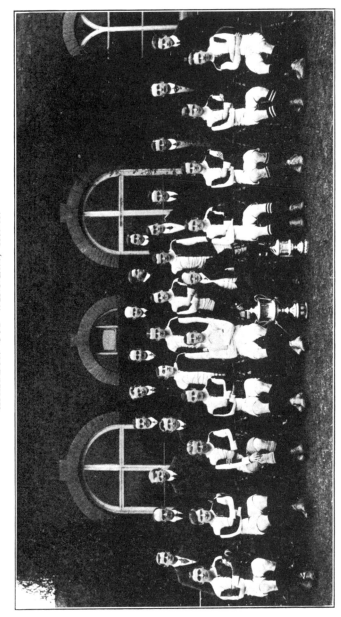

Second Row: Geo. Barlow, P. Oakes (Captain), T. Barlow, H. Jacques.
Front Row: R. Smith, W. Halliwell, S. Heaton, C. Armstrong, A. Selkirk, —. Kenyon (President), A. Royle,
W. Baron, J. Edwards, H. Gee.

# CHAPTER XXXVIII.

## THE EVOLUTION OF FOOTBALL.

*History of the Game. Description of Football. Sunday School players. Higher tone. Causes of improvement. Football encouraged by all ranks of society.*

It may be as one historian has said, " The origin of this violent game (football) is lost in antiquity, but there is much evidence of the attraction the game caused in the ' good old days.' "

It is recorded that in 1175 London Schoolboys played football. In 1314 King Edward II. forbade it, and King Edward III. found it necessary to enact a law against " football and similar foolish games." In 1389 Richard II. passed another Act prohibiting football playing, and the same Act was re-enforced by Henry IV. in 1401, and also by Henry VIII. A further reference to the ancient past is in the following description of our game :

Stubbs, the eminent antiquary says, " Concerning football playing, I protest unto you it may rather be called a friendlie kind of fyghting than recreation. For, doth not every one lye in waight for his adversarie, seeking to overthrow him and pick him on his nose, though it be on hard stones, in ditch or dale . . . So that by this means sometimes their necks are broken, sometimes their backs or legs, sometimes their noses gush out with blood, and sometimes their eyes start out." Another writer summed up his opinion of the game as " a bloody murthering practice rather than a felowly sport or pastime."

The descriptions given may be true of the days of " Merrie England," but they are in nowise descriptive of present day football.

It may be reasonably claimed that considering the thousands of games played every week, the number of players guilty of foul and reprehensible play is comparatively few. That statement is made after over twenty-five years' attendance at meetings.

Our honoured friend " Dick " Watson is often very indignant at the number of cases which arise from Sunday School football, his contention being that a higher standard of rectitude is expected from players of that class, than from players not connected with Sunday schools.

Whatever the cause, the fact remains that about 60 per cent. of the cases do arise from Clubs playing in Sunday School Leagues, despite the fact that some of such Leagues have made most praiseworthy efforts to raise the standard of play.

Since the Great War, 5,947 players have been dealt with at 450 Discipline Meetings specially held. This work involves much time and patience on the Members of the Council. Despite the figures named, the writer is firmly of opinion that the " tone " in football is higher, and that the number of players sent off the field is proportionately less than used to be the case.

What are the causes of this " higher tone ? " Firstly, the Junior Leagues are better organised than formerly, and the improved administration has re-acted on the players. Secondly, the players individually have a better conception of sportsmanship than used to be the case.

The old adage used to be, " if you can't beat him, cheat him." " If you can't win by fair means, win by foul—but win." But now-a-days an appeal has been made to " play the game," and the love of Britons for fair play has, and is, conquering, even in football.

Thirdly, we are indebted to the Referees' Societies for the work they carry on. The education of young Referees, the elimination of the dud and the ignorant, the stimulus to improve and achieve, have all helped to make football matches better controlled. The Referees' Societies are not striving for more pay and less responsibility, but they are organisations manned by honorary officials, and who do a good service in making known the finer points of the game, and in training up Referees.

These and other causes have resulted in a better atmosphere in and around our game.

No longer are we referred to as " Northern Hordes " or " Muddied Oafs," but footballers—Lancastrians or otherwise—are received and honoured by all ranks of Society.

Footballers—Juniors and Seniors—are no longer the " pooh-bahs " of Society. They indeed take their places in all phases of work—civic and national. No longer does " Dame Grundy " look askance at those who visit football matches.

Each Club now has its lady members and supporters, and football grounds are the rendezvous for all classes, sects and creeds.

Mayors, Judges, and even Monarchs themselves, have not thought it derogatory to their dignity to patronise our game, and join in our assemblies.

During Season 1927-28, Mr. Justice Swift attended matches at Hyde Road, Manchester ; and Ewood Park, Blackburn ; Mr. Justice Charles and Mr. Justice Hawke at Everton, whilst Mr. Justice Hawke accompanied by Lady Hawke attended the Lancashire Cup Final at Old Trafford, Manchester. Mr. Justice Hawke presented the Cup. Subsequently the President received a letter from the Judge's Marshall in which he says, " Mr. Justice Hawke and Lady Hawke enjoyed every minute of the game." It was to all of us a glorious finish to a great season and completes a history of which we are all very proud.

In the final season completing 50 years of record, Lancashire finished up in possession of The Football Association Cup, the Football League Cup, and the Football League Second Division Championship Shield.

**ROBERT CROMPTON.**
Blackburn Rovers F.C.

# CHAPTER XXXIX.

*Lancashire-born Players who became famous.*

In this Chapter you will see the names of eighty-five players who were Lancashire born and who have played for England in International Matches v. Ireland, Scotland, or Wales, together with a supplementary list of forty-six other players who, though not Lancashire born, yet played with Lancashire Clubs at the time they were " capped " to play for England.

The triumphs of " Bob " Crompton, the wizardry of " Jock " Simpson, the prowess of Crabtree, the doggedness of Joe McCall, the swerving of " Bob " Kelly, the cannon shots of Joe Smith, and the brilliance and characteristics of dozens of other players, all call for description and admiration, but our space is gone, and therefore the list compiled and referred to must speak for itself.

## LIST OF LANCASHIRE-BORN INTERNATIONALS WHO HAVE PLAYED FOR ENGLAND *v.* IRELAND, SCOTLAND OR WALES.

| Name of Player. | Where born. | Name of Player's Club. |
|---|---|---|
| Arthur, H. J. | Blackburn, | Blackburn Rovers. |
| Ashcroft, J. | Liverpool, | Arsenal. |
| Ashurst, W. | Wigan, | Notts County. |
| Baker, B. Howard | Liverpool, | Chelsea. |
| Balmer, W. | Liverpool, | Everton. |
| Bamber, J. | St. Helens, | Liverpool. |
| Bannister, W. | Burnley, | Burnley & Bolton Wanders. |
| Barton, J. | Blackburn, | Blackburn Rovers. |
| Becton, F. | Preston, | Liverpool & Preston N.E. |

| Name of Player. | Where born. | Name of Player's Club. |
|---|---|---|
| Berry, A. | Liverpool, | Oxford University. |
| Beverley, J. | Blackburn, | Blackburn Rovers. |
| Blackburn, F. | Blackburn, | Blackburn Rovers. |
| Booth, F. | Manchester, | Manchester City. |
| Bond, R. | Preston, | Preston North End. |
| Brindle, T. | Darwen, | Darwen. |
| Bradshaw, W. | Padiham, | Blackburn Rovers. |
| Bradshaw, H. | Liverpool, | Liverpool. |
| Bromilow, T. | Liverpool, | Liverpool. |
| Brown, J. | Blackburn, | Blackburn Rovers. |
| Bullock, N. | Monton, M/cr., | Bury. |
| Burgess, H. | Manchester, | Manchester City. |
| Butler, W. | Atherton, | Bolton Wanderers. |
| Booth, T. | Manchester, | Everton. |
| Chadwick, A. | Church, | Southampton. |
| Chadwick, E. | Blackburn, | Everton. |
| Chippendale, H. | Blackburn, | Blackburn Rovers. |
| Cowell, A. | Blackburn, | Blackburn Rovers. |
| Cox, J. | Blackpool, | Liverpool. |
| Crabtree, J. W. | Burnley, | Burnley & Aston Villa. |
| Crompton, R. | Blackburn, | Blackburn Rovers. |
| Davenport, J. K. | Bolton, | Bolton Wanderers. |
| Dawson, J. | Cliviger, Burnley, | Burnley. |
| Dewhurst, F. | Preston, | Preston North End. |
| Forrest, J. H. | Blackburn, | Blackburn Rovers. |
| Greenwood, D. H. | Blackburn, | Blackburn Rovers. |
| Hardman, H. P. | Blackpool, | Everton. |
| Healless, H. | Blackburn, | Blackburn Rovers. |
| Hibbert, W. | Golborne, | Bury. |
| Hodkinson, J. | Lancaster, | Blackburn Rovers. |
| Holmes, R. | Preston, | Preston North End. |
| Holt. J. | Church, | Everton & Reading. |
| Houlker, A. E. | Blackburn, | Blackburn Rovers, Portsmouth and Southampton. |
| Howarth, Geo. | Accrington, | Accrington. |

| *Name of Player.* | *Where born.* | *Name of Player's Club.* |
|---|---|---|
| Howarth, R. H. .. | Preston, ............... | Preston N.E & Everton. |
| Hargreaves, F. ..... | Blackburn, ........... | Blackburn Rovers. |
| Hargreaves, J. ..... | Blackburn, ........... | Blackburn Rovers. |
| Jack, D. B. N. ..... | Bolton, ............... | Bolton Wanderers. |
| Jones, H. ........... | Fleetwood, .......... | Blackburn Rovers. |
| Kelly, R. ............ | Ashton-in-Makerfield | Burnley & Huddersfield T. |
| Kingsley, M. ....... | Turton, ............... | Newcastle United. |
| Lofthouse, J. M. | Blackburn, ........... | Blackburn Rovers. |
| Longworth, E. ..... | Bolton, ............... | Liverpool. |
| Lucas, T. ........... | St. Helens, .......... | Liverpool. |
| Magee, T. .......... | St. Helens, .......... | West Bromwich Albion. |
| Marsden, Joe. ...... | Darwen, ............. | Darwen. |
| Marshall, Tom. ... | Withnell, ............ | Darwen. |
| McCall, J. ........... | Kirkham, ............ | Preston North End. |
| McInroy, A. ........ | Preston, ............. | Sunderland. |
| Mitchell, J. F. ..... | Manchester, ......... | Manchester City. |
| Molyneux, G. ...... | Liverpool, ........... | Southampton. |
| Mort, T. ............ | Kearsley, ........... | Aston Villa. |
| Nuttall, H. .......... | Bolton, ............... | Bolton Wanderers. |
| Page, L. A. ......... | Kirkdale, ............ | Burnley. |
| Parkinson, J. ...... | Bootle, ............... | Liverpool. |
| Reynolds, J. ........ | Blackburn, ........... | Aston Villa & West Bromwich Albion. |
| Rigby, A. ........... | Manchester, ......... | Blackburn Rovers. |
| Rostron, T. (Tot.) | Darwen, ............. | Great Lever. |
| Sagar, C. ........... | Turton, ............... | Bury. |
| Seddon, J. .......... | Bolton, ............... | Bolton Wanderers. |
| Settle, J. ............ | Bolton, ............... | Bury & Everton. |
| Shepherd, A. ...... | Bolton, ............... | Bolton W. & Newcastle U. |
| Silcock, J. .......... | Wigan, ............... | Manchester United. |

| Name of Player. | Where born. | Name of Player's Club. |
|---|---|---|
| Simpson, J. | Pendleton, | Blackburn Rovers. |
| Southworth, John. | Blackburn, | Blackburn Rovers. |
| | | |
| Taylor, E. | Liverpool, | Huddersfield Town. |
| Townley, W. | Blackburn, | Blackburn Rovers. |
| | | |
| Wadsworth, S. J. | Darwen, | Huddersfield Town. |
| Walton, N. | Preston, | Blackburn Rovers. |
| Ward, J. T. | Blackburn, | Blackburn Olympic. |
| Watson, W. | Southport, | Burnley. |
| Whitehead, J. | Church, | Accrington & Blackburn R. |
| Wilson, G. | Blackpool, | Sheffield Wednesday. |
| Wolstenholme, S. | Little Lever, | Everton. |
| Woosnam, M. | Liverpool, | Manchester City. |
| | | |
| Yates, J. | Blackburn, | Burnley. |

## LIST OF PLAYERS WHO HAVE PLAYED FOR ENGLAND v. IRELAND, SCOTLAND OR WALES, WHO THOUGH NOT LANCASHIRE BORN, PLAYED WITH LANCASHIRE CLUBS.

| Name of player. | Name of Club. |
|---|---|
| Abbott, W. | Everton. |
| Austin, S. W. | Manchester City. |
| | |
| Ball, J. | Bury. |
| Barson, F. | Manchester United. |
| Bedford, H. | Blackpool. |
| Boyle, T. W. | Burnley. |
| | |
| Chambers, H. | Liverpool. |
| Chedgzoy, S. | Everton. |
| | |
| Dean, W. R. | Everton. |
| Dewhurst, G. P. | Liverpool Ramblers. |
| Downs, R. W. | Everton. |
| | |
| Freeman, B. C. | Burnley. |

| *Name of player.* | *Name of Club.* |
|---|---|
| Geary, F. | Everton. |
| Goodard, A. | Liverpool. |
| Goodall, John | Preston North End. |
| Hardy, S. | Liverpool. |
| Harrison, G. | Everton. |
| Hilditch, C. G. | Manchester United. |
| Hill, J. H. | Burnley. |
| Hillman, J. | Burnley. |
| Howell, R. | Liverpool. |
| Jeffries, F. | Everton. |
| Latheron, E. G. | Blackburn Rovers. |
| Makepeace, H. | Everton. |
| Mew, W. J. | Manchester United. |
| Millward, A. | Everton. |
| Moffatt, H. | Oldham Athletic. |
| Mosscrop, E. | Burnley. |
| Plant, J. | Bury. |
| Puddefoot, S. C. | Blackburn Rovers. |
| Pym, R. H. | Bolton Wanderers. |
| Quantrill, A. E. | Preston North End. |
| Roberts, C. | Manchester United. |
| Roberts, F. | Manchester City. |
| Roberts, W. T. | Preston North End. |
| Sewell, R. W. | Blackburn Rovers. |
| Sharp, J. | Everton. |
| Shea, D. | Blackburn Rovers. |
| Smith, Joe. | Bolton Wanderers. |
| Spence, Joe. | Manchester United. |
| Sutcliffe J. W. | Bolton Wanderers. |
| Thornley, I. | Manchester City. |
| Turner, J. | Bolton Wanderers. |
| Wall, Geo. | Manchester United. |
| Waterfield, G. S. | Burnley. |
| Woodger, G. | Oldham Athletic. |

# CHAPTER XL.

## IN CONCLUSION.

*A Retrospect. The Association's Position, Past and Present. The Association Offices. Football and Charity. Jubilee Celebrations. Future work. Forty years onward.*

Our first difficulty was where to begin, and our last difficulties are, what to leave out and what to conclude with.

We have endeavoured to indicate fifty years' growth of football within the County, and we suggest that Lancashire holds a very honoured and exalted place in the Football world. That position has been won because Lancashire clubs were keen to achieve and maintain a high standard of play, and because players of our clubs compelled admiration, and in many cases secured deserved recognition.

The Junior Clubs, the Amateur and Sunday School Leagues, have all by their efforts helped in the great work of the development, organisation, and control of our game.

The Lancashire F.A. started in a small way, with few clubs and with little or no financial resources, but to-day, on the eve of its Jubilee, besides owning spacious Offices, it has £1,400 invested, has a Benevolent Fund of over £300, and has a full-time Secretary and Assistant.

The Association assists Schoolboy and Juvenile football, and more than once its influence has moulded the policy of The Football Association.

The Association Offices are premises of which we are justly proud. They are situate in the West End of Blackburn, and they comprise the Secretary's Office, a General Office, Board Room, two Committee Rooms, Storage

Rooms, etc. The rooms generally denote a football atmosphere, for there are many framed photographs of past and present Officers of the Association, photographs of numerous English International Teams in which many Lancashire players have played their part; photographs of Preston North End in the hey-day of their pomp and power, of the first F.A. Cup Final Tie played in the provinces, of the last F.A. Cup Final Tie played at Crystal Palace, of the first Final Tie played at Wembley, and of "Memories," which portrays all the Cup Final players from 1883 to 1926, these pictures being the gifts of Messrs. C. E. Sutcliffe, D. B. Woolfall, and J. Kenny, and of the Bolton Wanderers F.C. and Burnley F.C.

Only those who have been in close touch with the Association for a long period, can appreciate its changed fortunes, and its abnormal development.

The Jubilee finds the Association solvent, strong and firmly established; true, there will be those who will contend that the activities of the Association have been, and are, mostly in the interests of the Senior clubs. It is not our intention to argue that matter here—let this History speak for itself—but we wish to point out some of the things done on behalf of the noble cause of Charity.

Every August permission is given for collections or charges of admission at Practice Matches; and each Club has to make a Return of the receipts, also to whom they have been paid. From 1920-21 to 1927-28 inclusive, a total of £24,488 5s. 0d. was contributed to various Charities, such as Infirmaries, St. John Ambulance Societies, Clog Funds, Fresh Air Funds, Blind Societies, Orphanages, Press Benevolent Funds, etc. Further, there are many special matches played each season for the assistance of charitable institutions.

Organised Charity Competitions have done a wonderful work. The Burnley Victoria Hospital Cup Competition last Season contributed over £700 to the Burnley Victoria Hospital, and a total of £3,680 has been raised by this Competition since 1919.

The East Lancashire Charity Cup Competition (one of the oldest in the County) has contributed over £3,000 to different charities, and other organisations, such as the Bolton Charity Cup, James Thompson Charity Cup, Manchester and Salford Medical Charities, Ulverston and District Hospital Cup, Ulverston Trades Charity Cup, Standish Charity Cup, and the Westhoughton Charity Cup, have all raised creditable amounts.

In Chapter 15 you have the work of our own Benevolent Fund specially dealt with, and in addition to that, the Association has made many appeals for special causes, and no appeal was made in vain.

In 1883 over £40 was collected for the Altham Colliery Explosion Fund.

In 1899 over £400 was raised for comforts for the Troops serving in the South African War.

In 1902, £328 was raised for the sufferers of the Ibrox (International Match) Disaster; and in 1908, and again in 1910, substantial amounts were raised on behalf of the Maypole and Pretoria Pits Disaster Funds.

In 1914 over £3,000 was quickly secured and paid over to the Prince of Wales War Fund, whilst

In 1927, £1,133 9s. 5d. was speedily raised on behalf of those who suffered from the alarming and distressing floods at Fleetwood.

These efforts surely show that sentiment is not dead, despite the oft-repeated complaint that our game has become " sordid with commercialism."

What the Association, and its members, have been able to do for Charity, is a matter that surely should be mentioned in this collection of records.

This is our Jubilee year, and therefore we have endeavoured to pay tribute to all who have contributed to the work and success of the Association.

Our Jubilee Celebrations will take the form of a Banquet at the Imperial Hydro, Blackpool, on 9th October, 1928, which will be attended by the Right Hon. Lord Derby, and there will also be present other leaders of Lancashire, and leaders in Football.

On the following day a Jubilee Match will be played between a Team selected by this Association, and one selected by The F.A., and the game is to be played at Burnden Park, where Bolton Wanderers will do all they can to make the event a huge success, and we are certainly hoping our Lancashire Team will give a great exhibition of how International Matches should be played.

What of the future? Has the Association reached the zenith of its work? Has its best work been done? If that were so, then the Jubilee Banquet would be better described as a funeral feast. The Jubilee, surely, is not an occasion to mark the " setting sun " of the Association's activities, but it is an occasion to pay homage to those who have " gone before," to honour those who bear the responsibilities of governing our game, and at the same time to inspire the Association to greater efforts in the future.

In every phase of life there is progress, and so it is in football, and it may be the developments of the future may make great inroads in our resources.

Whatever the future, we to our Jubilee Banquet will go, and with sincere hearts raise our glasses to " the future success of the Lancashire Football Association," and if we were musically inclined, our voices would sing—

Forty years on, growing older and older,
    Shorter in wind, as in memory long,
Feeble of foot, and rheumatic of shoulder,
    What will it help you that once you were strong?
God give us bases to guard or beleaguer,
    Games to play out, whether earnest or fun;
Fights for the fearless, and goals for the eager,
    Twenty, and thirty, and forty years on!

        Follow up! Follow up!
    Till the field ring again and again
    With the tramp of the twenty-two men—
        Follow up! Follow up!

# THANK YOU!

The Compilers wish to convey their most sincere thanks to the following gentlemen, clubs and leagues for their valuable assistance.

For loan of photographs and blocks, for loan of publications, for information supplied, and for contributions, from: Messrs. A. Astley, Blackburn; J. W. Beardsworth, Blackburn; H. H. Birtwistle, Blackburn; W. E. Bracewell, Burnley; T. Bury, Darwen; L. Clarkson, Accrington; E. Clayton, J.P., Southport; T. Cragg, Manchester; G. Dale, Manchester; A. H. Downs, Bolton; H. Duckworth, Bury; F. Eastwood, Blackburn; E. Edwards, Liverpool; J. K. Fletcher, Bolton; R. Gowanlock, Manchester; B. C. Platt, Blackpool; Kenyon, Wigan; C. Francis, Blackburn; W. Garsden, Blackburn; J. W. Haworth, Turton; J. Holt, Reading; J. Kenny, Preston; T. Laithwaite, Parbold; E. Little, Blackpool; H. Makepeace, Liverpool; J. E. Mangnall, St. Annes; E. A. Morton, J.P., Liverpool; F. Martin, Blackburn; Gordon Nightingale, Blackburn; W. McCaffery, Blackpool; H. N. Patterson, Darwen; T. Paton, Bradford; T. Y. Ritson, Bolton; Ivan Sharpe, Manchester; J. Twist, Preston; H. Unsworth, Bury; The Allied Press, Manchester; A. Ward, Kirkham; R. Watson, Accrington; P. Winstanley, Hindley; Accrington Stanley, Atherton Collieries, Black Lane Rovers, Blackburn Rovers, Breightmet United, Bolton Wanderers, Burnley, Bury, Croston, Darwen, Earle, Everton, Horwich R.M.I., Lancaster Town, Little Lever, Manchester City, Manchester United, Marine, Morecambe, Oldham Athletic, Preston North End, Rochdale, Skelmersdale United, Southport, Turton, Westhoughton Collieries, and Williams Temperance; and our thanks are also due to all Clubs in The Football League.

Should we have overlooked anyone, no slight is intended; but we hope the above list is complete.

# YORE PUBLICATIONS

We specialise in the publication of Football Books with a bias towards the historical aspects of the game. We are pleased to receive details of any new books from prospective Authors, and any suggestions for reprints of out-of-print books that can be added to the 'Bygone Era Reprint' series. We issue a free Newsletter, three times yearly, giving full details of the new 'Yore Publications' titles (often at reduced prices for early subscribers) plus other books by other Publishers that fall within our ideals. Both League and non-League football books are included, as well as a number of unusual football videos.

### Current Titles include:

*THROUGH THE TURNSTILES (by Brian Tabner)*
An incredible book which analyses over 140,000 crowd figures to produce the average attendance of every Football League Club, for every season from 1888/89 to 1991/92! The book also relates the development of the game (angled towards attendances) from pre-League days to the 1990's. A chapter features **every** League Club, including record League crowd and best seasonal average attendance for each. Other sections give details of the best supported 'away' teams, season ticket sales over the years, etc. The book is well illustrated – from the 19th century to modern day – and will inevitably become a 'standard' reference book for serious statisticians as well as the casual reader. Large format (251 x 174 m.m.) hardback containing 208 packed pages. Cost £13-95 plus £1-70 post.

*REJECTED F.C. VOLUME 1 (Reprint) (By Dave Twydell)*
The 2nd Edition of this book – now with hard cover, minor additions, updates, corrections and re-set. This volume provides the comprehensive histories of: Aberdare Athletic, Ashington, Bootle, Bradford (Park Avenue), Burton (Swifts, Wanderers and United), Gateshead/South Shields, Glossop, Loughborough, Nelson, Stalybridge Celtic and Workington. The 288 well illustrated pages also contain the basic statistical details of each club. Cost £12-95 plus £1-25 postage. (Reprint of Volume 2, covering the remaining ex-League Clubs to follow at a later date)

......................................................

*REJECTED F.C.-THE VIDEO* ('Out of this League Productions' – Dave Twydell in association with Trans Video Productions). The video of the books (Rejected F.C. Volumes 1 and 2) has been very well received (*'Sportspages'* bookshop number 1 top selling video, February 1992). The 90 minutes running time will give several hours of repeated entertainment. Includes extensive film shots of the Grounds as they are today, interviews with many personalities related to these teams, relevant still shots to aid the telling of these Clubs' Histories... and an amazing collection of archive cine film (e.g. Ashington in 1924, pre-war New Brighton, Workington's last home Football League match, etc.). Each Club (starting with Accrington in 1888) is treated separately. Priced £12–99 (incl. VAT) plus £1–00 post.

*REJECTED F.C. OF SCOTLAND*
*Histories of the ex-Scottish League Clubs.*
*Vol.1: Edinburgh and The South. (By Dave Twydell)*
A follow on from the highly successful 'Rejected F.C.' books. The fascinating histories of ten Scottish ex-League Clubs (Edinburgh City, Leith Athletic, St.Bernards, Armadale, Broxburn United, Bathgate, Peebles Rovers, Mid-Annandale, Nithsdale Wanderers and Solway Star) have been comprehensively covered, complete with many illustrations, basic statistics and with particular attention to the Grounds of each club, especially those of the complicated three Edinburgh Clubs. You don't have to be a Scottish football fan to appreciate this book! 'Rejected F.C.' sold out quickly, but a reprint of 'Rejected F.C. of Scotland', is less likely. The book is a hardback and contains 288 pages. Cost £12–95 plus £1–25 postage. (Volumes 2 and 3 covering the remaining ex-Scottish League Clubs to follow at later date)

*MORE DEFUNCT F.C. (by Dave Twydell).* A follow up to the successful 'Defunct F.C.' book (Now out of print). Detailed and well illustrated histories of defunct Clubs – *Bedford Avenue, Lovell's Athletic, Romford, Rugby Town, Slough Centre and West Stanley* – including basic statistics. 230 pages. Only few copies remain. Price £6–75 plus £1 post.

........................................................

## PETERBOROUGH UNITED FOOTBALL CLUB
*The Official History of The Posh. (by Andy Groom and Mick Robinson)* After the most successful season in their history this 273 x 202 m.m., hardback (with full colour dust jacket) and printed on high quality paper will contain approx. 240 pages and will be a fitting tribute to 'The Posh'. Despite a Football League career of over thirty years, very little has been written about the Club. An extensive and well illustrated text section will detail the club's history from the earliest days, and the statistical section will contain the complete match and team details from the Club's formation in the early 1930's. Additional sections will include every Football League (and principal non-League) player who has played for the Club, plus a feature on the London Road Ground. Inevitably a 'must' for statisticans, Posh fans, and those who enjoy reading extensive and well written Club histories. Available December 1992. Cost £14-95 plus £3-50 postage.

## CARDIFF CITY F.C.
## THE OFFICIAL HISTORY OF THE BLUEBIRDS:
*(By John Crooks).* Large format (273 x 202 m.m.), cased (hardback) with a full colour dust jacket and containing 320 pages printed on high quality paper. Separate sections deal with the history of the Club in words and pictures (over 120 pages), an abbreviated 'Who's Who' section (every League player recorded), a section on Ninian Park, and the full statistics (including line-ups) of every major competitive match 1910–1991. A team group photo for nearly every season is also included. *("In the Super League of Club Histories" – South Wales Echo).* Cost £16-95 plus £3-50 post.

**THE IRONSIDES.** *A Lifetime in the League – Who's Who of Newport County (By Tony Ambrosen) ("Providing a hugely enjoyable read and a valuable reference book"* – South Wales Argus). Every player who appeared for the Club in the Football League is given a potted football and personal history, plus lengthy sections on the players during the Club's three periods in non-League football and details of all the Managers and Trainers. There are over 100 players' photos within this 224 page book. A 'must' for statisticians and those interested in this former League club. Price £8-95 plus £1 post.